The challenges and possibilities of the micro-entrepreneurs in Toronto

Romy Alegria

The challenges and possibilities of the micro-entrepreneurs in Toronto

Microfinance and microenterprise in the developed world

Éditions universitaires européennes

Imprint

Cover image: www.ingimage.com

Publisher:
Éditions universitaires européennes
is a trademark of
International Book Market Service Ltd., member of OmniScriptum Publishing Group
17 Meldrum Street, Beau Bassin 71504, Mauritius

Printed at: see last page
ISBN: 978-620-2-26775-5

Cape Breton University

THE ROLE OF MICROFINANCING AND MICRO-ENTREPRENEURSHIP IN THE ECONOMIC DEVELOPMENT OF THE CITY OF TORONTO: What are the challenges and possibilities?©

by

Romy Alegria

ABSTRACT

The purpose of this research effort was to understand why microfinancing and micro-entrepreneurship are not considered serious alternatives for alleviating poverty in the most depressed neighbourhoods of Toronto, Ontario. Research reveals that even though small businesses are the back bone of the Canadian economy, many resources get lost in the intricacies of bureaucracy, making it impossible for microentrepreneurs to benefit from any programs.

ACKNOWLEDGMENT

A project such as this does not happen via the efforts of one person alone. I was very fortunate to have the support of a few key people that I would like to acknowledge and personally thank here.

I want to express my sincere gratitude to Dr. Kevin MacKague, PhD, and Dr. Gertrude MacIntyre, PhD, for their invaluable guidance and patience in the development of this research project. I would also like to express my thanks to the Women's Development Network, in particular, Paula, Sadiyeh, Fadia, Omara, Fairuza, and Kenya, who opened up to me and took time to share their stories and dreams. Thank you to Sima, Lupe, and Alfonso who articulated their frustration and very personal sentiments to me, and to Jim Louttit, for awakening my belief in the power of entrepreneurship and microfinancing.

To the staff and faculty of the Shannon School of Business, thank you for helping to make this process both seamless and enriching, especially, Laura Syms who always got back to me within minutes and always with what I needed, and Dr. George Karaphillis, PhD, Dr. Michael MacNamara, PhD, Dr. Gregory Libitz, PhD, and Dr. John Conrad, PhD, for their continuous encouragement and guidance.

Finally, I would like to extend my deepest gratitude to my parents and dear friends for their patience over the past twenty-four months. Thank you for understanding when I needed to focus on my work and when I needed extra support to press on and realize my goals of completing this project and achieving my Master of Business Administration degree.

TABLE OF CONTENTS

CHAPTER ONE

1.0 INTRODUCTION

1.1 Problem Formulation

The number of well-paying jobs is shrinking, and unemployment rates are rising. Poverty brings delinquency, inequality, illiteracy, drug addiction, and creates a vicious cycle of more poverty. For many who come to Canada, survival skills are a crucial part of daily life. In fact, most immigrants posses micro-entrepreneurship skills. They are also resourceful, risk takers, courageous, and determined to succeed in their new home. In Toronto, 47% of newcomers and 37% of single mothers live under the poverty line (City of Toronto, 2016). There is a correlation between immigration, single parents, poverty, and resourcefulness. Current scholarship suggests microfinance and micro-enterprises as viable alternatives for promoting job creation, financial inclusion, and the economic development of neighborhoods or depressed locations.

For some micro-entrepreneurs, necessary financial support comes in various forms such as family, personal loans, credit cards, and payday loan stores. Many banks do not offer small business loans due to high operational costs and low returns. Indeed, obtaining financing in Canada can be expensive and cumbersome, especially when it is for a new business venture. Furthermore, business loans for recent immigrants are unheard of unless a person demonstrates liquid assets, real estate collateral, or has a guarantor. For many small businesses, immigrants, or disenfranchised people this means resorting to alternative measures such as a payday loan from one of the 200 payday loan stores located in the Toronto region. While this may seem like a reasonable solution, people who use payday loans often pay higher interest rates—up to 600% yearly— and lack full understanding of the

Canadian market (Pratt, 2014). If a micro-entrepreneur is resourceful and internet savvy, he or she might be lucky enough to connect with various micro-financing organizations or online lenders to secure a business loan at a reasonable rate of approximately 2.5% (Financial Post, 2017). However, the process of securing such a loan is often discouraging and frustrating. Not only is there an extensive list of requirements, such as a business plan, good credit score, two years of business experience in the city, and so forth, some micro-financing organizations lack resources, management, marketing skills, and their services do not always live up to their promises.

Clearly, micro-entrepreneurs face a variety of obstacles, even in the form of programs aimed at improving the economic well-being of communities. For example, the mandate of Toronto's Strong Neighbourhood Strategy 2020 (TSNS 2020) is to provide quality jobs and livable incomes for Torontonians (City of Toronto, 2016). Unfortunately, recommendations from TSNS 2020 focused on providing or extending welfare benefits lack specific actions, especially in terms of the promotion of or assistance to small businesses. This is despite increased worldwide acknowledgment of the economic contribution small businesses make to a countries' growth

1.2 Research Questions

A successful business environment requires the consideration and inclusion of micro-enterprises. It should promote new markets, partnerships, access to funds, technology, and training in such a way that its products become competitive, world-class, and ready to be integrated into the marketplace. In the City of Toronto, 55% of the business registrations are small business licenses. Regardless, microfinance and microenterprises remain underdeveloped.

Researchers, including Pedrini, propose the consideration of micro-enterprises and micro-financing as income generating activities more so than mechanisms designed to alleviate poverty in developing countries (Cao, 2012). However, in order for such approaches to become part of the poverty solution or to have an impact on it, some initial considerations and requirements must be established in terms of sustainability and obtaining a broader outreach (FAO, 2005). As well, financing products currently offered by micro-financing institutions need to be tailored to the requirements of the disenfranchised.

A series of questions arose as a result of the observations listed above. They are as follows:

- What are the impacts of microenterprise and micro-financing on developed nations?
- What is currently available for micro-financing in the City of Toronto? Who do these organizations serve and do they offer business training?
- What are the requirements to apply for a business loan?
- What role does microenterprises and micro-financing play in Toronto's economy?
- What is available to assist small and micro-entrepreneurs?
- Are small business owners prepared to make business decisions about market growth, financing, and distribution, and do they have a place they can go to for advice?
- And finally, the question driving this research effort, what are the challenges and possibilities of microenterprise and microfinance in the City of Toronto?

1.3 Summary of the Study

Chapter One explores poverty and job creation as it relates to micro-entrepreneurship. It discusses microfinance and microenterprises as viable alternatives for promoting job creation, financial inclusion, and the economic development of neighborhoods or depressed locations. It looks at the various problems business people face in terms of securing loans for microenterprises, including specific sources of funding for such ventures. Many questions are presented, including the main question driving this research effort: What are the challenges and possibilities of microfinancing and microenterprise in the City of Toronto?

Chapter Two provides a literature review of current scholarship as it relates to poverty in Toronto, and microfinancing and micro-entrepreneurship in Canada and the developed world. It reviews relevant definitions, entrepreneur traits, women and immigrant entrepreneurs, and worldwide trends.

Chapter Three describes the research methods used to complete the present study. It looks at the conceptualization of surveys, selection of research participants (for surveyss and in-depth interviews), data collection, and the outcome and generalization of survey answers.

Chapter Four discusses the research findings and responds to the question: What are the challenges and possibilities of microfinancing and microenterprise in the City of Toronto? It underlines that the challenges facing microenterprises are ultimately linked to microfinancing. As well, because there is a strong distinction between micro-entrepreneurship and small businesses, individual policies should be created and applied. Other findings include a lack of applied business fundamentals geared toward the development of a small/micro businesses, a lack of commitment by some women to micro-entrepreneurship for fear of losing welfare benefits, and finally, although microfinance in Toronto does exist, these programs do not match the needs of Toronto's micro-entrepreneurs.

Chapter Five concludes with suggestions for strengthening the micro-entrepreneurship and microfinancing environments. It has been demonstrated there is an immediate and profound need for Toronto's institutions and citizens to partner-up in the creation of thriving communities via the implementation of mentorship program, marketplaces, and government programs that reach those most in need of assistance.

CHAPTER TWO

2.0 LITERATURE REVIEW

2.1 Introduction

Micro-entrepreneurship and microfinancing are regarded as valid options to alleviate poverty in the global south. So, why has the global north not considered promoting a sustainable environment to create more microenterprises that may reduce poverty levels in developed cities? To better understand the situation, it is important to examine current scholarship related to the topic. Hence, the following theoretical analysis of the most recent scholarly papers, academic journals, and book reviews will assist in determining the relationship between poverty, women, micro-enterprises, and micro-financing. It will also provide an explanation of pertinent information that shaped the survey and interview questions used for this study.

This chapter begins by examining poverty in Toronto using statistics from *TO Prosperity: Toronto Poverty Reduction Strategy* complemented by analysis of other world-class cities (City of Toronto, 2015). It is followed by a discussion of the current micro-entrepreneurship environment, entrepreneurs' traits, women and immigrant as entrepreneurs in developed economies, and the state of micro-financing in Canada, including its possibilities, focus, and how it serves depressed communities in the global north.

2.2 Poverty and Unemployment in Toronto

In the City of Toronto, approximately 375,000 people live in poverty. Of this number, 46% are recent immigrants, 37% are lone female parents, and 33% are racial groups (City of Toronto, 2015). Generally, Torontonians with lower-incomes mostly live in districts classified as Neighbourhood Improvement Area(s) (NIA) due to the fact that they lack certain conditions that involve the provision of robust urban infrastructure, access to the right jobs, recreation, and community disenfranchisement (Appendix A). The Toronto Poverty Reduction Strategy (2015) pays particular attention to the physical surroundings of NIAs for the purpose of creating economic opportunities, promoting healthy lifestyles, and participating in social development. However, the median monthly income for people living in these neighbourhoods is CAD820 for single adults, CAD1,465 for single parents, and CAD2,055 for two-parent families (City of Toronto, 2016).

Bigger cities, such as Toronto, hold the largest wealth concentrations due to attracting young professionals and numerous immigrants. However, Toronto also has the highest level of unemployment sitting at 7.1 percent (Government of Canada, 2017). Although almost five thousand small businesses and 48,300 new positions were added to Ontario's job market this year (Canadian Press,2017), annual earnings still do not match the cost of living in the city; social assistance barely covers rent and food, leaving almost nothing for other needs.

Some think a basic, guaranteed income, and cash in pocket is the solution to poverty. The City of Dauphin, Manitoba, is a vivid example of a successful attempt to ensure that nobody falls below the poverty line (Bregman, 2017). Ontario's premier, Kathleen Wynne, believes that raising the minimum wage will make "a world of difference" for families (Schnurr,2017). According to Statistics Canada, minimum wage in Ontario will increase 32% over the next 18 months from CAD11.60 to CAD15.00 per hour in 2019 (Government of Ontario, 2017). While more money may seem like a cure-all for poverty, some have concerns that an increased minimum wage will negatively impact low-income families and businesses. For example, the Financial Accountability Office of Ontario

(FAO) (2017) forecasts that a rise in minimum wage will cut around 50,000 jobs. According to Shum (2017), "since the income gains would not be concentrated on low-income families, raising the minimum wage would be an inefficient policy tool for reducing overall poverty".

In neighborhoods such as Regent Park, Thorncliffe Park, Oakridge and Moss Park, poverty rates are above 50%, the highest in Toronto (Alliance for a Poverty Free Toronto, Children's Aid Society of Toronto, Colour of Poverty Colour of Change, Family Service Toronto, & Social Planning Toronto, 2015). The average income for families living in these areas is CAD34,825; in the richest neighborhoods, the average is CAD423,850, thereby increasing the disparity, social exclusion, and marginalization of the population (Landeu, n.d.). The fact that many newcomers are settling in marginalized and excluded neighborhoods, with limited access to public infrastructure and services, makes them more vulnerable to rest of the population. Figure 1 indicates that recent immigrants, people with disabilities, seniors, youth, and ethnic communities are more likely to live in poverty in Toronto (Community-Wealth.org, 2015).

Figure 1

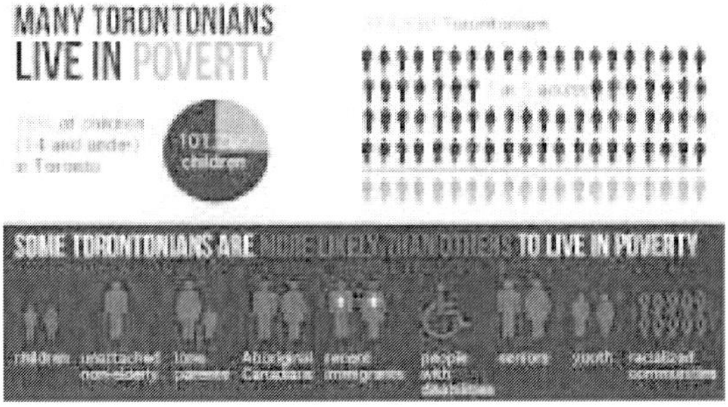

Numerous metropolitan areas are facing difficulties in terms of job creation but almost half of the working-age population of Toronto is comprised of immigrants; they comprise more than half of the working-age employees in Toronto (OECD, 2006). Young immigrants account for 27% of the working employees. With limited opportunities for education, a stable address, transportation to attend interviews, restricted access to computers, phones, and a social network, the chances of thriving in the city are low. Hence, a higher minimum wage is not a solution to poverty. In fact, the FAO (2017) estimates that the higher minimum wage will raise the total labor income (after adjusting for price inflation) by 1.3 percent by 2019.

2.3 Micro-entrepreneurship

According to the *Business Dictionary (n.d)*, an entrepreneur is "someone who exercises initiative by organizing a venture to take benefit of an opportunity and, as the decision maker decides what, how and how much of an excellent service will be produced." This past century, Schumpeter (Cox, n.d.) was the economist most associated with the term indicating an entrepreneur is an innovator who drives the "creative-destructive" process of capitalism and the change agent in the economy creating new markets or new ways of doing things. However, new theories expanded to include the concept of social entrepreneurs defines them as a rare breed of entrepreneurs whose objective is enterprise success instead of wealth creation (Dees,1998). The term "microentrepreneur" describes the owner of a microenterprise defined as a "sole proprietorship, partnership or corporation that has fewer than five employees and lacks access to conventional loans, equity, or other banking services" (Government of U.S.A.,2006).

The term "micro-entrepreneurship" was popularized by Nobel Prize recipient Muhammad Yunus primarily due to its close relationship with microfinancing. In Canada, businesses are defined by the number of employees. A small business has 1 to 99 employees, this includes sole proprietorships, partnerships, and self-employed individuals. Hence, a microenterprise is a subset of a small business. Usually a family business, sole proprietorship, or partnership has fewer than five employees (Government of Canada, 2015).

2.4 Micro-entrepreneur Worldwide

Martine Durand, Director and Chief Statistician for the Organisation for Economic Co-Operation and Development (OECD), indicates that in Europe small entrepreneurships are the drivers of economic growth (OECD, 2017). Worldwide, small and medium-sized businesses represent 99% of all businesses, and 85% of new jobs created (Khana, 2015). The United Nations University suggest three main reasons for this growth (Naudé, 2011). First, the reliance on mass production has given way to knowledge-driven goods and services, and an entrepreneurial economy. Second, innovative entrepreneurship is leading the way in terms of sustainable growth, especially in emerging economies like the BRICs – Brazil, Russia, India, China. Finally, donors are shifting aid towards more private development efforts and promoting youth entrepreneurship.

With economic trends indicating that start-ups (small businesses) account for about 70% of new jobs globally—and in some emerging markets as much as 91%—movements like Entrepreneurs Unite (EU) in the United Kingdom (UK) are currently advocating for government policies that empower entrepreneurs (Dell,2017; Entrepreneursunite.co, 2017). For instance, one proposal endorses four fundamental considerations in the development of an entrepreneurship environment: access to markets worldwide, access to capital, access to technology, and access to talent, thereby removing immigration barriers to hiring high-skilled individuals worldwide.

In Canada, this same sector accounts for approximately 85% of all newly created employment (Douglas, 2013). In Ontario, during the financial crisis of 2008 and 2009, as the number of welfare cases soared, small businesses created nearly 16,000 jobs for the province (Government of Canada, 2012). Approximately 30% of the country's GDP is attributable to small businesses (Government of Canada, 2012). Small businesses operate in professional services, agriculture, forestry, fishing, and hunting, and they are the backbone of the Canadian economy, even though in many cases, they do not have payroll deductions; such companies are comprised of one person, and employees are family members or contract workers. In 2015, of the 1.14 million businesses existing in Canada, 97.9 were small businesses and 54.9% were considered microenterprises, which means they employ between 1 and 5 people, and more times than not, lack both the credit history and collateral needed to secure a loan (Government of Canada, 2012). As a result, over 80% of start-ups are established with the assistance of personal financing (Government of Canada, 2016).

According to Statistics Canada (2011), Ontario has 407,175 small (1-99 employees), 8,437 medium (100-499 employees), and 1,189 other (500+ employees) businesses, for a grand total of 416,801 small and medium-sized enterprises (SMEs) or 36% of all SMEs in Canada. Start-up SMEs often lack both the credit history and collateral to secure a loan. Over 80% use personal financing, 45% use credit from financial institutions, and 19% receive trade credit from suppliers (Government of Canada, 2016). As the baby boomer generation gets older, it is projected that many of their small businesses will be passed down to their heirs. Needless to say, this will involve a massive transfer of assets—estimated at between CAD 1-trillon and CAD 4-trillon in Canada alone, thus creating more expansion in the development of small businesses in Toronto (Blackwell, 2015).

2.5 Characteristics of an Entrepreneur

In *The Portable MBA in Entrepreneurship*, William Bygrave was the first person to characterize the exact qualities of an entrepreneur (Bygrave & Zacharakis, 2010). He also identified the 10 qualities of a successful entrepreneur. They are as follows:

1. **Dream:** Entrepreneurs have a vision of what the future could be like for them and their businesses. And, more importantly, they can implement their dreams.
2. **Decisiveness:** They do not procrastinate. They make decisions swiftly. Their swiftness provides a key factor in their success.
3. **Doers:** Once they decide on a course of action, they implement it as quickly as possible.
4. **Determination:** They implement their ventures with total commitment. They seldom give up, even when confronted by obstacles that seem insurmountable.
5. **Dedication:** They are totally dedicated to their business, sometimes at considerable cost to their relationships with their friends and families. They work tirelessly. Twelve-hour days and seven-day work weeks are not uncommon when an entrepreneur is striving to get a business off the ground.

6. **Devotion:** Entrepreneurs love what they do. It is that love that sustains them when the going gets tough. And it is the love of their product or service that makes them so effective at selling it.

7. **Details:** It is said that the devil resides in the details. That is never truer than in starting and growing a business. The entrepreneur must stay on top of the critical details.

8. **Destiny:** They want to be in charge of their destiny rather than depend on an employer.

9. **Dollars:** Getting rich is not the prime motivator of entrepreneurs. Money is more a measure of their success. They assume that if they succeed they will be rewarded.

10. **Distribute:** Entrepreneurs distribute the ownership of their businesses to key employees who are critical to the success of the business. (Bygrave & Zacharakis, 2010).

2.5.1 Female micro-entrepreneurs

It is estimated that small and medium-sized enterprises owned by women contribute an estimated CAD160 billion to the Canadian economy (Government of Canada, 2017). The sector has grown 35% since 1999, and start-up rates are increasing. Statistics from North American and European countries show that, on average, 30% of entrepreneurs are women: Denmark 21%, France 22%, Germany 26%, Norway 27%, Sweden 26%, UK 26%, and USA 63% (Mayoux, 2001). Businesses owned by women are primarily in the service industry, information, health care, administration, and recreation.

According to Moore and Buttner (1998), “A female entrepreneur is a woman who has initiated a business, is actively involved in managing it, owns at least 50 percent of the firm, and has been in operation one year or longer". Worldwide, many studies recognize that women in business are necessary for the long-term development of the family, neighborhood, and country (Iganiga,2008). In the global south, “women play a vital role in the economic development of their families and communities. However, women are subject to gender-related discriminations especially in lower middle countries" (Iganiga,2006). Gender discrimination is uncommon in Canada (MacDonald,2014). In reality, the simple fact that micro-financing is not targeting women as borrowers shows that the gender ratio of borrowers is equal. There are very few programs targeting women, and the idea that if you help women, you help the whole family are themes that characterize the entrepreneurship environment for women (MacDonald,2014).

Canada's Prime Minister, Justin Trudeau, is a self-described feminist, and as such, his government is very mindful of empowering women and recognizing their economic contribution. Trudeau firmly believes that when a woman's value is not fully recognized, “it is a missed opportunity for many countries that could benefit greatly from the economic contributions of women" (Harris, 2017). However, what is most commonly seen is the promotion and celebration of powerhouse women, and to a lesser degree, woman who work just to benefit their communities and society. In the documentary, *The New Economy* (2016), filmmakers Melanie Wood and Trevor Meier look at the Thorncliffe Park Women’s Committee to find who how they came to be and what they do to organize their weekly markets. Happy Healthy Women (2017) is an example of a successful collective that began as a small group of women discussing life and business, and grew to be an organization with15 branches and more than 7000 members. Karam Kitchen is a newly formed group of female Syrian refugees living in Hamilton and already contributing to the development of the community via catering. In August 2016, the Women's Development Network was established for the purpose of providing peer support, skills development, and social enterprise opportunities to women in Regent Park and surrounding areas. The group's mission is to promote the full participation of women in social and economic life. Its vision is to build a strong network, and provide diverse opportunities for women to build confidence, trust, and a sense of well-being through community participation (Garcia, 2017). In one way or another, women in Toronto are participating, at their own pace, in the economic development of their neighborhoods.

2.5.2 Immigrant micro-entrepreneurs

Many people become entrepreneurs by default because there are no other options (Storm, 2008). For others, including immigrants, entrepreneurship may be more appealing due to the possibility of a higher income. The lack of certifications, licenses, or language skills may limit employment opportunities, thereby making start-ups more appealing to immigrants (Economist, 2009). Immigrants tend to be risk-takers, it is not clear if it is by nature or necessity; they are ambitious and resourceful, always looking for ways around difficulties such as language barriers; they are perseverant and have business ideas when others run for cover, aka, full-time employment (National Immigrant Forum, 2016). Take Germany for example; 2015 saw an unprecedented spark in immigrant entrepreneurship—44% of new business belonged to foreigners (Economist, 2017). From 2010 to 2016, under the guidance of then Prime Minister David Cameron, Britain became one of the most entrepreneurial countries with a record of 608,110 business registrations in one year (Economist, 2016).

Immigrant entrepreneurs operate in a variety of ways. Some see a market opportunity and find a way to get it done with or without a business plan. Others are like captains of a ship, driven by an inner force and refusing to take "no" for an answer. They usually open businesses in underserved retail markets and neighborhoods showing a "higher tolerance for risk. Immigrant entrepreneurs are known for seeking out labor-intensive business opportunities with low start-up costs and low barriers to entry all of which are accessible within underserved markets (Tobocman,2015)".

According to the Toronto Region Immigrant Employment Council, by the late 2000s, 19% of Canada's immigrants were self-employed (Wayland, 2011). However, these numbers are lower in the Greater Toronto Area (GTA) because of higher opportunities for paid employment and the age of immigrants living in this locale (Wayland, 2011). According to the *Globe and Mail(2011)*, 33% of immigrants in 2000 pursued self-employment because of a lack of job opportunities in the paid labor market; of those admitted into Canada in 2010, 42% were immigrant entrepreneurs; 71% of immigrants who are voluntarily self-employed are motivated by entrepreneurial values, versus 59% among their Canadian-born peers. Nonetheless, even the most motivated entrepreneurs still require the most basic supports in order to successfully establish a business in Canada, from creating a business plan, to expanding professional networks, and securing the necessary capital (Wayland, 2011). On the other hand, a study conducted by the European Commission on Immigrant Entrepreneurship (2005) suggests a holistic approach to entrepreneurship,. It insists that training, regular advice, social capital, and the facilitation of business funding and working spaces are best practices for entrepreneurs to thrive.

2.6 Microfinance

2.6.1 Definition of microfinance

According to Investopedia (2017), "Microfinance is a type of banking service that is provided to unemployed or low-income individuals or groups who otherwise have no other access to financial services. Ultimately, the goal of microfinance is to give low-income people an opportunity to become self-sufficient by providing a way to save money, borrow money and get insurance".

2.6.2 Group lending

Joint-liability groups are a main innovation of microenterprise development (Schreiner, 2003). Group lending is a synonym of joint-liability. It happens when a group of people come together and borrow money for economic activities. In northern countries, development enterprises spearheaded by women are promoted as key elements to decrease welfare budgets and unemployment; however, group lending is not a common practice (Mayoux, 2001). A group of borrowers form a group among themselves and the microfinance institution gives a loan to the group. The group appoints a leader, and each person is responsible for the loan taken by any member of the group. If any one person in the group defaults, the other group members will have to pay their share (Finance Cosmos, 2009).

Mark Schreiner (2003) offers four reasons of why group lending has struggled in North America. First, the country has weak social capital; there is no need for permanent or long-term economic relationships. The market is faceless; there is no need for assistance or trust between neighbors. Second, a lack of diversity means that small towns would not have the capacity to support many similar businesses. Third, microenterprise programs do not enforce joint liability. Fourth, if people have good credit they still can get individual loans through credit cards or costly loans.

2.6.3 Microfinance in the developed world

The European Commission stated that 7% of the European population (35 million) is estimated to be under-banked with limited access to financial services. In the United States (US), this same situation involves 14% of the total population or 45 million people (Giusti & Estevez, 2011). In Canada, 4.2% of the population does not have access to basic banking accounts mostly because of bank fees, inaccessible locations, and unavailable credit (Buckland, 2012). Hence, even in a developed country, a person with no income also has no access to bank loans or good interest rates. The for-profit organizations certainly would not entertain this type of client, and the non-for-profit businesses would only have limited capacity to assist.

The purpose of microfinancing activities in northern countries is to pick up the slack and "fill a void" left by larger banking institutions (Macdonald, 2014). That being said, studies on microfinancing are still young and poorly delineated in the global north (Pedrini et al. 2016). Between 2014 and 2015, lending and borrowing worldwide grew to 16% or 130 million customers and USD96billion (Global Envision, 2006). The first microfinancing organization in Canada, Calmeadow, before closing its doors in 1999, had 922 borrowers and a portfolio of CAD2.3 million in micro-financing loans (Frankiewickz, 2001). Today, online micro-lending and related organizations have flourished but access to current portfolio sizes is non-existent—

the industry is new and small. There is, however, coexistence between the use of conventional financing options and microfinancing.

In developed countries, microfinancing growth has not been as dramatic as in the global south; between 3% to 4% (World Bank, 2013). Worldwide, industry growth is up 12.6% with a USD87.1 billion loan portfolio (Perron, 2016). Unfortunately, some of the most common challenges faced by immigrant entrepreneurs are language, knowledge of business culture and practices, and securing financing (Sim, 2015).

Financial exclusion plays a big role in urban development; people with lower incomes have a complex relationship with fringe and mainstream banks. This is evidenced by: unaffordable high-interest rates, low supports (e.g., customer service training for the segment, financial literacy curriculum, etc.), and the absence of loan products in micro-mini amounts (Buckland, 2012). Newcomers to Canada and youth both represent segments of the population who are economically poor, and do not yet have the knowledge, skills, and experience to navigate Toronto's financial sector in order to make informed financial decisions and avoid unscrupulous organizations, such payday loans. Payday loans are time-limited and often come with quick approval and no credit checks.

2.6.4 Differences in micro-financing practices

The following are differences between microfinancing practices in the two global economies.

- The Players

Microfinancing institutions cannot take savings from customers because they are not a depository institution, authorized bank, or financing institution with a banking license (Pedrini et al., 2016). Microfinancing organizations are usually non-profit or publicly subsidized (Macdonald, 2014). Therefore, there is limited profitability from interest on loans, savings, insurance fees, transfer services, and other financial products than what is garnered in for-profit businesses.

- Lending Methodology

Since its inception, micro-financing promoted join-liability and peer lending practices. Muhammad Yunus, founder of the Grameen Bank, worked with groups of 15-20 women using the idea of solidarity as the guarantee for loans instead of credit history (La Roque,2015). Although borrowers from some parts of the global north expressed an interest in centers where they could exchange ideas, get support, feedback, as well assistance with financial difficulties, lending practices remained the same and the inclination towards individualized loans continued (Bredberg, 2011; Macdonald, 2014). PARO Center for Women's Enterprise is the only institution in Canada that provides lending support, as a group, to like-minded women.

- Target

Traditional microfinance targets the poorest, unbanked, women and small business entrepreneurs. In the developed world, the target market is individuals, male and female, excluded from formal financial markets because they lack collateral (Spotton, 2011). MacDonald (2014) recognized that even though very few organizations explicitly target women as borrowers, this particular market represents the biggest portion of microfinance borrowers in Canada. Bredberg and Ek (2011) identified low to moderate income households, regardless of gender, as the target market. They also found that in developed economies, job creation, especially after the financial crisis, is the primary goal of micro-financing institutions.

- Size of Loans

It is said that giving credit in the developing world for as little as CAD10 is worth 60 times more than in developed countries (DEKI, 2017). As the cost of goods is higher in the global north, loans range from USD5000 to USD25,000 (Pedrini et.at,2016). Most microfinance organizations provide loans to a maximum of USD10,000 (Macdonald, 2014). What is worth mentioning is that the cost of processing loans is the same regardless of size; it is one of the reasons why banks do not make small loans. The resources required for a CAD50 loan is the same as for a CAD1000 (Microfinanceinfo.com, n.d.).

- Gender

An important caveats of microfinancing is the significant gender disparity in the developing south—almost 73% of all microfinance borrowers are women (LaRoque, 2015). In Canada and other parts of the global north, the movement is gender-free and neutral (for the most part) because inequality is not considered a larger problem in developed countries (MacDonald, 2014). Also, there is no evidence that gender borrowing or targeting women would improve the movement (Bredberg, 2011).

2.6.5 Purpose, relevance, and desirability of microfinance

Pedrini et al. (2016) established five primary goals for microfinance activities in developed countries: job creation, promotion of microenterprises, financial inclusion, social inclusion, and empowerment of specific target groups. The purpose of microfinance is to serve the poor and unemployed, and to reduce the financial burden of social welfare on national and local governments (Pedrini et al., 2016). Having access to financial services could be crucial for depleted communities, and micro-financing could play a significant role in poverty reduction, particularly when regular financial and banking remains rigid and restrictive (MacDonald, 2014). Micro-enterprise and micro-financing are not a panacea for poverty alleviation, but it is required. In developing countries, it is common to link microfinancing impacts with female empowerment. Nonetheless, in the global north, both men and women are empowered through their participation in microfinance programs (Bredberg & Ek, 2011). This is because such programs provide a venue for capacity building and transition toward a new beginning through the support and networking of micro-entrepreneurs (Rebekah, 2010).

The demand for microfinancing is growing but the supply is not enough. In Canada, MacDonald (2014) predicts that industry will continue receiving significant subsidies, not only from government grants, but by a growing number of commercial banks interested in becoming more socially responsible.

2.6.6 Role of the microfinance in Canada's economy

While literature that explores microfinancing in the developed world is limited, the sector has transformed itself into a multi-purpose program that provides loans for business expansion, skills development, and other programs and services (Gomez & Santor, 2001; Spotton Vusabino, 2008; MacDonald, 2014). MacDonald (2014) identified 60 microfinancing organizations in Canada, each of them responding to a particular category and service. However, her definition deferred to what it is known as classic microfinance in which micro-entrepreneurs are served with loans and financial products.

The following is a summary of MacDonald's (2014) classification:

- Classic Microfinance

Microfinancing organizations in Canada are twenty in total, located mainly in the business centers of Quebec, Ontario, and British Columbia. These organizations provide small loans for the start-up or expansion of a self-employment venture. They have a structure similar to the classic model of micro-finance pioneered by the Grameen Bank. In these organizations, the number of volunteers is higher than paid employees. They serve low-income people with financial barriers and no credit history. Money is lent to individual borrowers; however, 5% of loans are based on peer-lending practices where eligibility is determined according to character, business plan, skill set, training, and the borrower's finances. The average loan is CAD9000 with the maximum set at CAD45,000.

- Upgrading and Training Skills Funds/Loans

Upgrading and training skills funds/loans could be considered a subset of classic Canadian microfinance as its beginnings date back to the mid-2000s. Organizations that specialize in this type of financing have less volunteers than traditional microfinance groups simply because they remain small in scale, scope, and outreach. Loans are provided to immigrants for upgrading and training. An individualized lending model is used for money disbursement, and eligibility is determined using a "character-based" method, requiring personal and financial household information, a business plan and skills, and previous training for qualifications. The maximum loan amount is CAD15,000. These types of organizations are funded mainly by government and rely heavily on partnerships with other not-for-profit/community groups.

- Developmental Lending

Programs under this category are not considered micro-financing organizations but rather developmental lending programs. There are two particular programs that serve Canada North including the Northwest Territories and Nunavut. They are the Community Features Development Corporation (CFDC) and Community Business Development Corporations (CBDC). Each has a small number of paid employees (two staff members) and five volunteers. There is no specific target, borrowers become members, and they are strictly male borrowers rather than females. Approval is based on a person's character with high reliance on borrower finances and financial statements due to the size of the loan. The most significant difference between developmental microfinancing and classic microfinance is the size of loans. Developmental loans can go as high as CAD100,000, and repayment rates are between 90- 99%. The loans are mostly used for start-ups or expansions, and funding comes from multiple levels of government.

CHAPTER THREE

3.0 METHODOLOGY

3.1 Introduction

This present research effort uses a mix of both qualitative and quantitative data adapted from a model developed by Robert E. Stake and Helen Simons, well-known case-based researchers (Soy,1998). In-depth interviews attempt to provide an understanding of the interviewees' demographics, background, family, and the impact micro-enterprise and microfinancing has had on their lives. These interviews also contain information about the current state of the business affairs; their knowledge, application of business fundamentals, compromise with entrepreneurship, and the future as they see it.

The quantitative side of the study employs a survey prepared to find answers about the type of business, industry, associated legalities (i.e. if the firm has a license or not), the entrepreneur's knowledge and training to handle business decisions, the need and awareness of microfinancing, and the challenges and conviction to continue being a small business owner.

The tools used to conduct primary research include professional journal reviews, observations, surveys, bibliographies, magazines, reports, and publications. It involves insights from ten in-depth interviews and survey results garnered from micro-entrepreneurs and small business owners. Also included is a description of current small lending products, such as online credit offers, payday loans, and microlending options for micro and small businesses. The microlending section features four mini case-studies of Futurepreneur, Access Capital Fund, Rise Asset Development and Catapult Microloan as the only options that strictly provide loans to those most in need. The rest of the chapter is as follows:

- Conceptualization of Interviews and Surveys
- Selection of Research Participants
- Data Collection
- Conclusion

3.2 Conceptualization of Interviews and Surveys

This study includes four in-depth interviews (see Appendix B) with the leaders of Sister-to-Sister Beauty Group, Innovation Jewellery Group, and Regent Park's Sewing Collective and Knitting Group; all part of the newly formed Women's Development Network. It also includes three in-depth interviews (see Appendix C) with the following small businesses owners: the owner of Riince, a manufacturing company that has designed a new utensil for measuring and washing quinoa, removing the contaminant and making sure that quinoa and other seeds are not lost down the drain. The creator of an online platform that connects Spanish speaking people with Latino businesses. The owner of an online radio who broadcasts live using a Facebook platform. Three final interviews round out the total to ten. Two interview subjects assist with the development of emerging economic groups, and one subject has expertise in developing microfinancing-microenterprise models worldwide.

The research survey seeks to provide an initial diagnostic of the micro-entrepreneurial situation in Toronto. It provides insight into of the types of businesses entrepreneurs engage in, and if they are compliant with obtaining required registrations and licenses before starting operations. The survey looks at business acumen to carry on business practices, and training and general knowledge of the industries they are involved in, including product creation, marketing, distribution, and taxation. It also addresses operational skills and challenges, resources for obtaining financing and microfinancing, and the opinions of microentrepreneurs regarding what initiatives should be implemented and supported by government in order to support their development.

3.3 Selection of Research Participants

Research participants were chosen from an extensive database of people in business, entrepreneurs, sales representatives, and so forth. Thus, it was necessary to take certain steps before finalizing the list and deploying the survey. First, employees working for corporations, commission based people, and sales representatives were removed from the database. Second, companies that matched the survey's target group—microenterprises or small business with no more than five employees—were identified. In some cases, it was necessary to make a few phone calls to confirm the number of employees. Also, the companies needed to be located in the Greater Toronto Area. Third, entrepreneurs' email addresses were confirmed. Questionpro, an online research company, was used to confirm the validity of email addresses, and to deploy the survey. As a result, the survey was sent to 96 businesses.

The second part of the study consists of in-depth interviews with small business owners. Before selecting the subjects, it was necessary to determine three variables: location, background and business activity. First, it was important to make sure that all of the selected business owners work and have their businesses activities in one of the three different Neighbourhood Improvement Areas: Regent Park, Kingsview Village - The Westway, and Downsview - Roding - CFB. Second, all the interviewees are Canadian citizens; 90% are first-generation immigrants, and one is a second generation immigrant living in Toronto since she was a child. Finally, all businesses highlighted in this study have been up and running for more than one year. It is important to note that one of the selected businesses is in the final stages of endorsing a new invention. Although it has yet to be sold in stores, the product is over a year old and is currently under production. Each of these businesses represent a different industry: manufacturing, services, applications/websites, knitting, beauty parlor, sewing, jewelry, and communications. The interviews were conducted in two separate languages, English and Spanish, and the meeting locations were a mix of workshops, coffee shops, and the Toronto Reference Library.

Looking at those who were interviewed for this study, business owner Sima, inventor of "Riince", is a second generation immigrant of Indian descent with experience in business management and innovation. Her business is at the initial stage and currently has a landing page online but no physical location. Alfonso, from Colombia, is the sole proprietor of "Latinto", an online application that connects Latin businesses to the Latin community. Lupe is the owner of Kbuenaradio.tv, an online radio with live transmission through Facebook platforms. Leaders from the Women's Development Network include: Fairuza, from the Regent Park Women's Sewing Collective; Omara, leader of Innovation Jewellery Group; Rafia, from Sister-to-Sister Beauty Group; and Kenya, from the Knitting Group. Other interviewees are Ranee L. from OCAD who also helped shape the Regent Park Women's Sewing Collective; Paula G., Community Capacity Builder from Yonge Street Mission, and finally, Jim Louttit, District Governor for Rotary Club and Vice-President of the Toronto International Microfinance Summit.

3.4 Data Collection

3.4.1 Survey design and launch

After testing some web-based survey companies, QuestionPro.com was chosen to complete the task. This online company allows ten free questions per survey; however, it was essential to upgrade the service so that thirteen exploratory questions could be sent out. Although the service was not free, the fee was justifiable and reasonable. QuestionPro.com provides the software to create the survey; however, the researcher must create it and test it manually. There is an option to upload questions and email addresses but this feature has a separate cost. The company also provides different templates for an invitation survey letter. All in all, the program is very user-friendly. One click on "create a new survey" and the system prompts you to type in the question and suggests item buttons that are correctly categorized. Using a mix of multiple choice questions, box matrix tables, and star ratings, provided the survey with both flexibility and agility.

The survey included an invitation cover letter (see Appendix D) explaining the purpose of the research and thanking participants for their input. The questions are concise and direct. The expectation is no more than seven minutes for completion, and that was also explained in the invitation letter. The survey was deployed the last weekend of August 2017. It was a long weekend, and responses started to come up five days after. It was fundamental to make some phone calls encouraging people to respond. Finally, the poll was closed on the 15th of September to process results. The completion rate is 20.8 with 0 dropouts and 17 additional views without action.

3.4.2 Managing completed surveys

It is a fundamental part of this research to create charts and prepare a detailed analysis of the results. Questionpro.com provides the option to download raw data, but for extra features, such as queries or tables, there is an additional cost. The tables and charts contained in this study were organized manually and offline. Predefined answers and the number of questions facilitated the analysis.

3.4.3 Outcome and generalization of surveys

The data used in this research study was collected comes from different sources including a survey and in-depth interviews. The data was tabulated and combined. A close examination of responses, with consideration of the development stage of the business, provides valuable insight to the many challenges micro-entrepreneurs face when creating, growing, and sustaining a business.

For the in-person interviews, it was necessary to record all conversations for accuracy. During the interviews, when other questions arose, it was important to dig deep to extract additional and valuable information that was probably not addressed in the initial survey or preliminary interview questions. Note taking was also helpful to facilitate later analysis, and to triangulate data that would aid in strengthening the findings.

3.5 Conclusion

The research objects in this present case are essentially seven small business owners and microentrepreneurs at different stages of development—the germinated social enterprises at Regent Park, an innovator looking to promote a unique kitchen tool that will help people cook better and lead healthier lifestyles, a communicator, and an app developer. A combination of research methods and data gathering made it possible to understand the different contexts in which these people perform their daily business activities. As a qualitative-quantitative exploratory study, it was fundamental to understand the backgrounds, histories, and business expertise of these unique individuals.

CHAPTER FOUR

4.0 RESEARCH FINDINGS

4.1 Introduction

The purpose of the present research is to identify the challenges and possibilities of micro-entrepreneurship and microfinancing in the City of Toronto. As the literature review shows, the Canadian government if quite confused when it comes to differentiating between a small business owner and microentrepreneur. Worldwide, micro-enterprises are tiny businesses that start at home , hold a business registration, and do not have more than five employees. Employees are mostly family members and eventually, some contractors; there is no difference in the volume of annual sales. To facilitate comprehension, this present research effort adopts USAID's (2002) definition that states that micro-entrepreneurship is “an informally organized business activity which is owned by and employs poor people, including the micro-entrepreneurs and any family workers and is not engaged in crop production”.

Canadian businesses can be classified into three different groups: small businesses, medium sized businesses, and large business corporations. As a subset of small businesses, collective grassroots groups should also be included; however, the majority, although community based, do not hold any license. Small businesses, as well as collective grassroots groups, are full of challenges and possibilities, but the emerging groups are the most vulnerable, facing tremendous challenges to thrive. The second group relevant to this study are businesses that are more mature (in some cases), have set up shop, have years of expertise, and annual sales surpassing the one hundred thousand dollars, but still, have no more than five employees.

4.2 Challenges of Microenterprise and Microfinance in Toronto

4.2.1 Understanding what is a small business verses micro-business

It is unknown exactly what differentiates a small business from a micro-business. With no clear understanding of what a micro-business is, how is a society to address concerns, identify challenges, provide solutions, and advocate for policies? In Canada, businesses are classified as corporations, sole proprietor or partnerships, and cooperatives based on the number of employees. For example, a business with 1-99 employees is considered a small business. Clearly, the first challenge is understanding that microenterprises are a subset of small businesses but with an entirely different meaning, goals, background, and so forth. For instance, where do we fit microbusiness that emerge from grassroots, are creating income opportunities for people in the community, and has not for profit motives per se? If the Women's Development Network chose to register and pay taxes as a social enterprise, legally, they would have no option. Evolving from a woman's support group, the Woman's Development Network thrived and grew in this incubator-type environment. However, in reality, if it decided to register and pay taxes, it would have to choose another type of business and have this social enterprise activity at arm's length of another organization. Not only would this limit their ability to generate profit, it would cancel out any possibility to raise funds from investors and run the enterprise as a business (O'Connor,2014).

Business goals are another difference. Small entrepreneurs have a profit orientation while micro-businesses are looking to generate income for the first time and at least a minimum wage (Fairuza, 2017). Sometimes the collective sewing ladies receive between CAD3 to CAD5 after sales for a very labor intensive product. Scalability related to the number of employees and capital investments differs as well. While small businesses invest to grow their activities (and capital requirements may be high), microentrepreneurs have limited scalability because the resources are completely dependent on gifts and donations.

Emerging auto-denominated "social enterprises" are lifting people out of poverty, creating incomes that contribute to a family's budget, building social capital and capacity, and developing work skills in immigrant women who have never worked in their lives. The table below illustrates the most remarkable differences between small and micro businesses.

Table 1

ENTERPRISE LEVEL	SMALL BUSINESS ENTREPRENEURS	MICRO BUSINESSES/SOCIAL ENTERPRISES
Legal status	Registered as small business	Unregistered
Ownership	Sole proprietor, partnership, limited liabilities, corporation	Collective
Scale	Small-scale regarding number of employees, mostly 1 to 5 employees but with may have higher levels of capital investment	Micro-scale regarding investments and production, usually money comes from donations, gifts, own resources. The number of members/employees often goes up to 5 or 6.
Type of business	Niche product/ manufacturing, for instance, hardwood flooring, brick engineering panels, frame installations	Services: well-being, sewing, cooking, beauty parlor, employment development, environmental or social purpose
Technology	Maybe be capital and labor intensive	Little technology and labor intensive
Business goal	Economic and Profit orientation	Survival/complement to family income
Financing	Use of savings, family, friends and personal loans	Not a priority especially at initial stages of formation. Relying on donations and gifts

Labor	Paid, contractors or family distribution income	Underpaid
Business background	Some business training, short courses, previous experience in the field, or university background	None, in some cases not even work experience outside family home
Access to information	Through friends, former managers, colleagues, guaranteed access to support network	Insufficient access to resources/no knowledge of information center or outside support
Ethnicity	Combination of Canadians born and immigrants	Mostly immigrants

4.2.3 Lack of business fundamentals

- Business Plan

Every business starts with an idea that needs to be summarized into a business plan, or at least, a business model canvas, to guide operations and marketing activities, to explain how to organize resources, and the strategies to reach the set-up goals. A business plan is a roadmap of where the entrepreneur wants to go with the firm. Unfortunately, survey responses were disconcerting; entrepreneurs are doing business without having the necessary knowledge of how to run a business, or how to bring the money. Also, many believe that a business plan should be a long document with specific details about operations, finances, and marketing. However, according to Sima, there is no need for a microentrepreneur "to have a 300-page document (business plan) prepared in colors printed, but a business model canvas gives a perfect picture of what they want to do”. A business plan is a fundamental, mandatory tool that helps to organize customers, identify target markets, competitive advantages, and finances, and control and monitor the progress of the business.

Business planning addresses a company's mission and vision, as well as something as basic as whether or not a target market is appropriate for a new initiative. At the Regent Park sewing collective, determining the target market proved to be somewhat conflicting. They produced the products but were not getting the sales they wanted. After three years in business, they decided to launch themselves at the Double Take (storefront) initiative. A student from a business school approached them and explained what they needed to do to be in business (Paula, 2017).

Some businesses continue without direction or understanding of how to create revenues even though the resources and capabilities exist. As Lupe, owner of Kbuenaradio.tv, explained: "Kbuenaradio.tv started as a school project for my daughter. She created a broadcasting program for the school, and we bought the first equipment for her microphone and a radio mixer... after seven years, the radio does not generate revenue, it is a money sucker, we need to allocate money from other business to maintain the radio operations" (Valdivia, 2017).

- Legalities and Taxes

Registering a business is not always a priority for smaller entrepreneurs. The Regent Park collective sewing group, auto-denominated as a social enterprise, is an unregistered operating business. The ladies maintain an income generating activity without holding a formal business registration and license. The group decided now is not the time to set up a legal company. They may consider registration once they can generate enough profits and become independent from the support of the Yonge Street Mission. Kbuenaradio.tv has a recognized brand within the Latino community. Although it organizes events, and produces daily programming, it is not formalized as a business. On the other hand, the more established small entrepreneurs do not confirm hundred percent registrations either. Approximately 40% of respondents avoided answering the question, "Are you formally registered?

Table 2

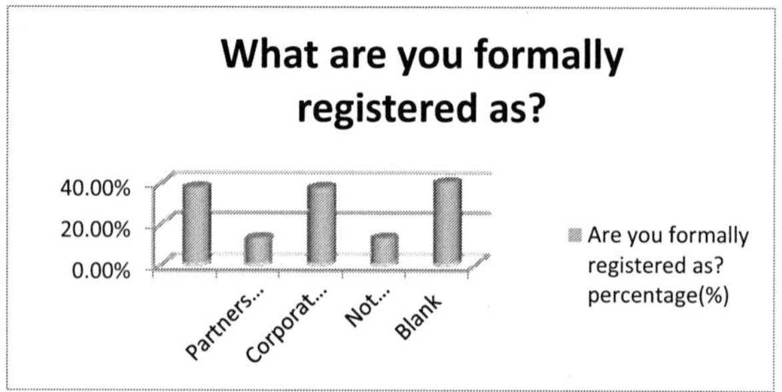

Further research reveals possible reasons why micro-businesses and small entrepreneurs choose not to be officially registered. The City of Toronto has a list of trades, profession, and business that required a license. To access one, the prices average CAD300 approximately, and can be done with a simple click. Is it the price, or the lack of information on the benefits, obligations, and tax implications, that make people shy away from formally registering their companies? It seems like wrong information or the absence of correct information forces businesses to operate "under the table" or marginally, without license or registration. Transactions are on a cash basis, so part of the fear comes from the idea that when a microentrepreneur starts making more money or getting more jobs they will lose government benefits. According to Fadia (2017), "...every time you start working, the rent increase almost 30 to 35percent...they (Ontario Works) take 33 percent approximately of your earnings. So what comes in your hands after working 30 to 40 hours a week is just CAD100 or CAD200 increase. That is why, all these community members of Jameson, Regent Park, Moss park community what they want to do is either go to Ontario works, or they want to do cash (jobs). They know as they get the cheque (from work) everything will increase, rent will increase, income tax will increase, and child benefits will be close" (Fadia, 2017).

- Product and Market

Those interviewed for this study are very comfortable with product creation. They know how to create beautiful products, but sometimes they don't know what the market needs. Producing hats, bags, or bed sheets does not mean they know what the customers or students want. They also do not have a good understanding of the Canadian market. These ladies have simple ideas, and they sew that way, but at the same time, the expertise among them is incredible. A partnership with the industrial design program at the Ontario College of Art and Design (OCAD) allowed the ladies of the Regent Park Sewing Collective to choose from a series of student designs to create products that respond to market needs. Although this helped, the ladies' initial reaction was to choose the most simple patterns and designs, and to ignore anything that could have produced a more sophisticated sample for exquisite markets ready to pay a high price (Rene, 2017).

Table 3

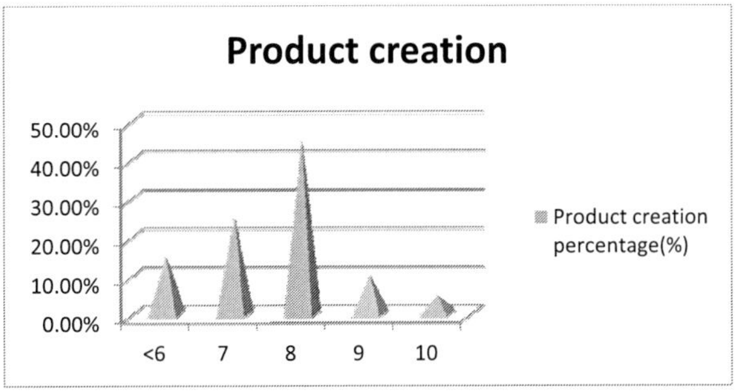

More than 40% of respondents agreed they are comfortable with product creation; they understand the core business and the products. The issue, however, is the market and where to get customers. They forget to ask, who is going to be the client? What is the target market? Where are they located? What is their demographics? Are they willing to pay the tag price? Does the product require a niche market? The Women's Development Network decided to open up a storefront using the VIP section of the Double Take (second-hand store) to display their merchandise. Items range from CAD10 to CAD35 dollars, and it also helps that the store is located in the Regent Park neighbourhood.

- New Marketing Approaches

Depending on the type of business, marketing strategies should be tailored to the target market. Businesses owners need to understand market trends, requirements, and the price customers are willing to pay for products. Millennials, as a target market, do not like to be sold, hence, the marketing approach for them is soft sales. Developing a marketing campaign will require the use of different tactics. For instance, as a way of launching Riince, Sima contacted bloggers and websites that promoted "clean living" to introduce her product as it supports a healthy lifestyle. The product, a three in one kitchen tool, makes it easier to measure, wash, and handle small grains such quinoa or seeds. Sima decided to invest her time and money in explaining and educating healthy eating bloggers on the benefits of her products until they got the "buy-in". Unfortunately, the WDN does not know how to use marketing techniques. They are doubting about selling in at Regent Park, community churches, and market fairs, because potential clients do not like to pay for products made by them (Fairuza, 2017). The segmented market is poorly defined, and according to the survey results, almost 60% of the entrepreneurs scored lower than 6 (average) in marketing and customer knowledge.

Table 4

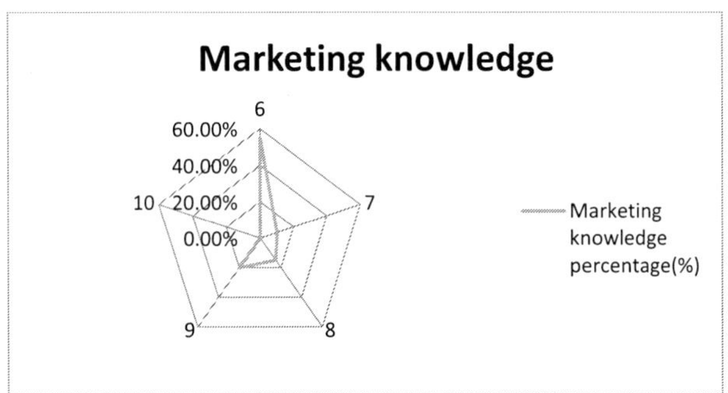

Truth be told, the WDN lacks vision when it comes to their clientele. Items are priced to match market prices but the neighborhood where they mostly sell is not willing to pay the costs. Potential clients fall in the lowest-income range and this creates disappointment and confusion because although the collectives would like to sell to their neighbors, their work-intensive products make it difficult for them to reduce their prices.

- Operations

Operations address the skills and strengths of the entrepreneurs to carry out business activities. How do they do their job? How do they maximize resources to create a product? What is involved in product manufacturing? These tasks could start at home, or in workshops. In total, 60% of the survey respondents believe they have above average knowledge of how to run their own businesses. This is understandable because the companies have no more than five employees and many of them have previous experience. Most probably, many learned the trade for a few years and then made the leap of faith to create their own personal companies.

Table 5

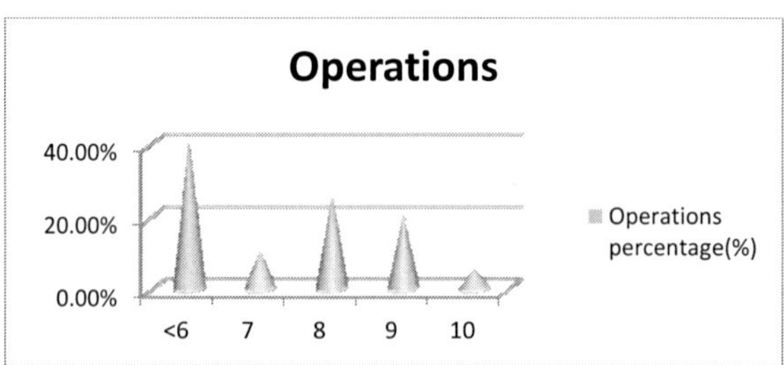

When it comes to grassroots organizations, the operations are not daily and many times under supervised. The WDN uses tools and supplies provided by the Yonge Street Mission, and the projects are very specific. They get together, once a week for two hours, during sewing classes, where they sew and teach new students. Unfortunately, it can take up to an hour just to set up the workshop, bring out the supplies (fabrics, zippers, and thread), and cut out the patterns (Fairuza, 2017). As a result, many try to finish the work at home using their own sewing machines and sometimes the quality is too poor and projects need to be redone.

The current inventory consists of 30 bags, 100 stockings, 30 scarves, 15 infinity scarves, 20 small pouches, and 10 aprons, all with a total face value of CAD2,870 approximately. Products made in the last twelve months have not been sold. Low turnover and accumulated inventory is an indication of weak sales. The products are stored in one of the closets at the Yonge Street Mission where they also kept a safety box with some cash and sewing tools.

4.2.3 Self-improvement and innovation

Canada's Innovation and Skills Plan introduced an agenda to convert Canada into in a world-leading innovation economy that creates jobs and grows the middle-class (Government of Canada, 2017). The plan supports the creation of well-paying jobs and developing professional skills to strengthen a well-educated workforce. According to Sima (2017), “Self-employment is an owner-operator type of business that is not entrepreneurship that is not what the innovation economy is trying to fund".

Entrepreneurial training lead by community organizations is often lacking in business skills and trade skills: "when I presented my business plan to the worker center, he told me I knew more than him . . . he did not help me with anything" (Alfonso, 2017). Entrepreneurs are constantly challenged by the demands to keep up with technology, improve trade, and learn more about how to sustain a successful enterprise. According to the survey results, 55% of business owners are willing to receive business training online. On a positive note, the WDN is always searching for people to assist them with improving their business capabilities and knowledge.

Table 6

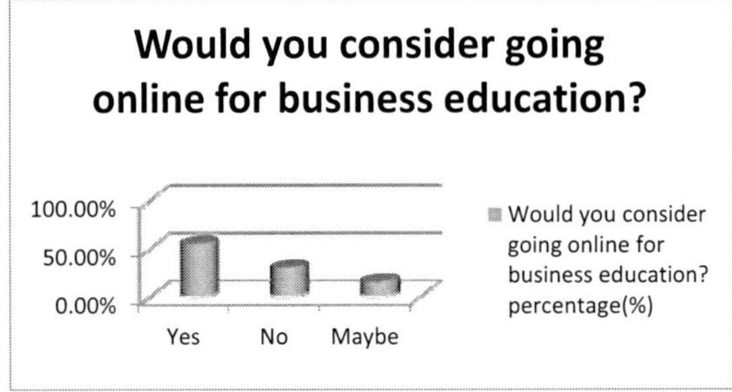

4.2.4 No commitment to entrepreneurship

The research produced two very distinct responses to entrepreneurship itself. On the one hand, 100% of the survey respondents agreed that having their own business is a good source of income, demonstrating decisiveness and strength despite continued challenges.

Table 7

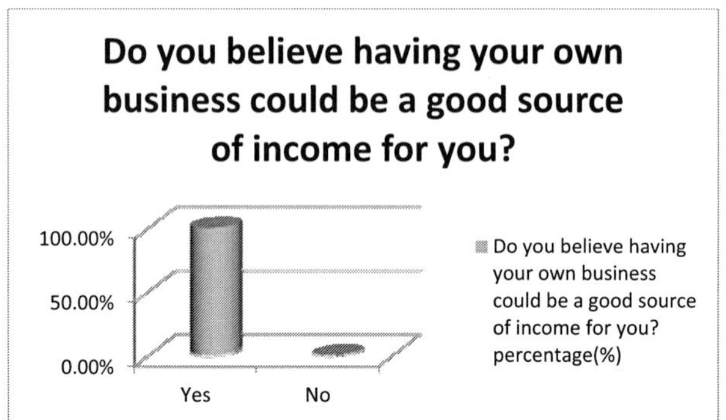

These small business owners are committed and determined. Mr. Fix It (2017) responded “it is now and has been (my source of income) for 15 years”. They are also in charge of their own destinies. As Raul (2017) explains, it is “more work but freedom is an asset”. Small business owners are doers, “it is very hard”, but they continue to plow through daily—failure is not an option (Sonom, 2017). Alfonso is passionate about his business; he knows that money is the result of his efforts. He is devoted to his business, even when he is tired, but as a digital marketing consultant, he provides free advice on some occasions. He explains, “client asks many questions, demand top of the line service but they do not like to pay” (Alfonso, 2017). Still, he pursues his business with conviction. He enjoys the freedom and flexibility of not having to work in an office from 9 to 5 rather than focusing on the uncertainty of the next contract. He gets frustrated but he knows the money will follow.

On the other hand, the WDN lacks the same determination and understanding of what it means to be an entrepreneur. This group has been in existence for more than five years, but it was only two years ago that they began thinking of turning their activities into something that generated income. In reality, this initiative responded to two forces: funding for programs was coming to an end, and YSM was trying to stir the group into becoming self-sustainable. Previous to this, the ladies spent two years learning and perfecting their craft in knitting, sewing, computer applications, beauty treatments, jewelry making, and building social capacity. Last year, when revenues started to pick up, a kind of agitation ensued with some of the ladies suggesting that a salary from WDN would be a better option. Their dedication continues as they work tirelessly to complete projects but at the risk of using personal time and family resources.

An entrepreneur needs to wear many hats until the business takes off. Until reaching that point, an entrepreneur must act as a sales person, packager, distributor, manager, accountant, and so on. The WDN does not understand marketing principles, and feels quite overwhelmed with current inventories and earnings for all the work done. After sales, the net income fluctuates between CAD3 to CAD5 per hour, which is not "enough to keep them happy and motivated" (Fairuza, 2017). It is not about wanting to do or not to do the job, people are committed, but they need incentives, and they do not know what to do without creating disappointment and hopelessness.

There are very specific markets and selling techniques for the goods produced by the WDN. As mentioned, an entrepreneur is also a salesperson, but to be in front of clients when you have never had to work or sell something is nerve-racking, especially for people who speak English as a second language. Many ladies do not want to work in the storefront, but if these shifts are not filled, there are no sales (Paula, 2017). The right market niche would be willing to pay a premium for products that benefit the community that produces them. Kenya (2017) from the knitting group said, "they asked me, have you made this hat? And I said I made it, so they pay me 25 dollars for it", but it is not enough to convince them. Omara (2017), leader of the jewelry group, said they would like to become independent or register the business one day in the future but "the team does not sell enough to be a business or to supplement the income at home". So, they remain dependant on YSM in order to continue working. To others, this is a hobby: "I retired, I have money... but want to have a place where to go and give back to the community" (Kenya, 2017).

Language barriers are a huge issue that deters the ladies from dealing with new customers (store front) or expanding the market outside their ethnic community. Alfonso partnered up with a friend because his language skills did not provide opportunities to do more business. When the partner left, he was stuck working in the Spanish community. He signed up for English as a second language class but did not last because of concerns with making money to feed his children and other emotional burdens.

When a business is formalized, there are many the legal responsibilities, including taxes, that one must comply with. This may add bureaucracy but it also allows the business to take advantage of other opportunities provided by the municipality or province. However, some would rather hide their income and assets to continue receiving public assistance and living informally. As stated by Paula (2017), "they get a little bit of money from the government, it is not much, they live in social housing, they get a (tax) break, they rent a space based on how much money they make, so they said we don't want to report more income, or we don't want to start making more money than x amount because we are going to lose our benefits". Without a clear understanding of how the system works, and how government can help small business owners rise from poverty, these types of businesses will remain informal and unregistered. The "system isn't set up to actually support people to move out of the (welfare) system. Our system is penalty based; you make money then you are going to get penalized. So why would you want to work" (Paula, 2017).

4.3 Micro-financing as an Option

Worldwide issues, such as financing, are one of the hardest challenges facing small enterprises. An entrepreneur requires knowledge of financial products and where to access them. For example, debt financing can help a business purchase technology for marketing, expansion, and innovation, but where do you get it? How much do you get? How do you apply for a business loan? There is a certain amount of knowledge that is quite necessary if a business is to be successful, and the need for business financing is demonstrated with 63% of small business respondents confirming that funding is an issue in terms of growing their business.

Table 8

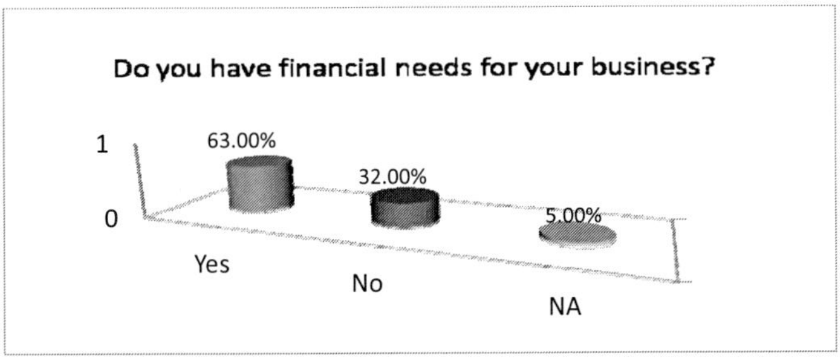

If financing is a requirement for small companies and the banks, as stated in the literature review, are not providing loans to entrepreneurs, what institutions are filling the void? The answer can be found online. Over the past two years, Thinking Capital and CIBC partnered up to offer small business loans from CAD5000 to CAD300,000. The minimum requirements for securing a loan are being in business for at least six months and generating sales of CAD7,000 monthly (Shecter, 2015). Unfortunately, they do not finance start-ups. For those type of requirements, an "angel investor" may be willing to invest in the business as long as the entrepreneur is ready to give up some equity. Examples of angel investors may be found on the television program *Dragon's Den)*. Hence, it is not the absence of options that poses the problem, such as in developing countries, it is the options with strict limitations that do not alleviate financial issues faced by micro and small business.

Microfinancing organizations are very limited in Toronto—there are 4 in total. But according to the survey, only 21% of the respondents had even heard of them. That means almost 80% of business owners were oblivious to the existence of microfinancing organizations in Toronto.

Table 9

Have you heard about micro-financing organizations in Toronto?

	Yes	No
	21.00%	79.00%

Of the number of business owners surveyed, only 5% had received a microfinance loan. The reasons for this vary. According to Sima (2017), "If a person chose to be an entrepreneur has to be prepared for the hardship of having no money to pay, needs to be ready to make sacrifices, cut expenses, restructure finances, or maybe move in with family or friends just to save cash". Being an entrepreneur can be quite difficult and financially exhausting, and while there are programs that help business owners deal with this, if you do not even know they exist, how can you take advantage of them?

Table 10

There are some who believe that an entrepreneur should be ready to invest their savings, ask banks or family and friends for loans, or use other personal sources such credit cards, lines of credit, or mortgage their properties to start their businesses. But the solution is not that simple. As businesses grow and improve production, innovation and exporting requires extra funding. In Sima's case, her father was able to finance her new business. She used her own resources to register the Riince patent and invested CAD3000 to get started. Riince is a new kitchen utensil for measuring and washing small seeds, removing contaminants, and making sure quinoa and other seeds are not lost down the drain. To create the first prototype, she invested just CAD100, but the second prototype cost CAD1000 because it was professionally done. In building the real model she wanted to be more efficient with money. After paying for some new drawings, she went to China and spent CAD6000 to build one model. Sima's invention is now ready for market. The first inventory run cost between CAD35,000 to CAD40,000, but it is her father who is funding this step.

Even applying for loans or grants can be overwhelming for the most experienced small businesses but mainly for the emerging entrepreneurs: "don't really know much about what is currently being offered, we applied for a grant for Fairuza and husband, they used to have a construction company, have some tools and wanted to hire some young people, she offering transportation and equipment for training them but they didn't get approved for the grant. I helped her to fill out the form, but we don't know how to fill out that grants. I'd love to do it. But I don't know how to. I don't know what the city resources are or how to access it. It feels like a big puzzle, too much work, they are so complicated . . . the process (acquiring grant and loans) feels complicated and discouraging" (Paula, 2017). Consequently, these small organizations have given up looking for additional funding.

Nonetheless, most people in Canada have access to financial services, including loans and credit cards via personal banking that may be used for business purposes. The problem is that many entrepreneurs do not understand the benefits of financial products. For example, the WDN set up a chequing account, not for its advantages, but because they wanted to accept credit card payments for customer purchases. A chequing account is a requirement of a point-of-sale machine, but no transactions have been posted; they still keep their money in a safety box in one of the closets at YSM. They do not understand, nor has it been explained, that besides protecting money from theft, fire and other threats, a checking account is also helpful in keeping track of money in and out. Not every entrepreneur has the same experience when it comes to financial matters, but more than 60% of the respondents acknowledged their incompetence when it comes to financial matters.

Table 11

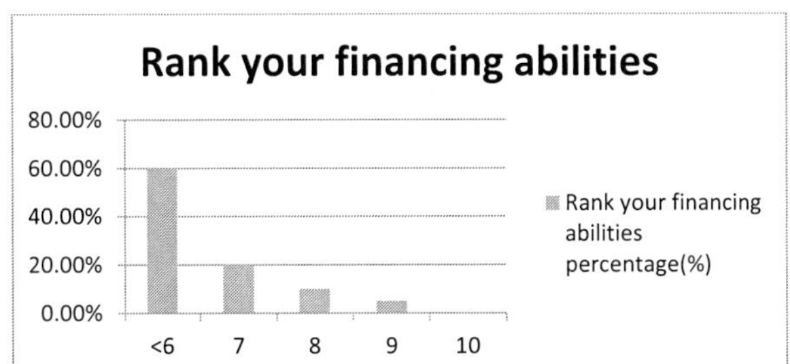

Basic financial literacy for small entrepreneurs on how to budget, set goals, and make use of financial products is indispensable when it comes to overcoming poverty and growing their businesses. To complete the development of his new application, Alfonso is short CAD5,000. His past financial decisions have affected his capacity to access personal or business loans; his bad credit excludes him from mainstream banks. The application he developed has great potential, but it is stuck for lack of cash. He had never heard about microfinancing, except for payday loans. However, he is not willing to pay 500% interest per year interest on a payday loan that offers debt consolidation. Thus, he struggles between paying debts, finishing his application, and surviving in the Toronto. This has created a never ending, vicious circle.

4.3.1 Micro-financing offers

Strictly speaking, there are five micro-lending organizations in Toronto. There are also more that 200 payday loan stores, a handful of Canadian online lending stores, and more than 10 American online lending stores, all of which are supposed to serve the financial needs of micro and small business entrepreneurs. This is what they are supposed to do; the reality is quite different.

4.3.2 Online credit offers

Online organizations such as Mogo, Prudent Financial, Lending Arch, and ThinkingCapital target the small to medium-size enterprise market. They offer loans at lower interest rates, one to three-year repayment options, and quick and accessible online approval and funding. They do not provide business advice, coaching, training, or financial literacy. They also require a year of activities. Minimum loans are CAD5000 and can go up to CAD35,000. According to their websites, loan approvals can take up to twenty-four hours, and funds are deposited into a client's chequing account. Quick, hassle free, and good rates but just for business owners. Today, the online lending community is expanding primarily due to the launch of FINTECH. FINTECH or financial technology programs are advanced financial alternatives to old transactional operations such online payments, peer-to-peer transactions, alternative lending, and crypto-currencies. However, these services are not provided to micro-entrepreneurs or those who live under Ontario Works. For instance, Thinkingcapital only accepts applications from business that have been in operation for at least six months and over CAD7,000 in gross sales (Zeeshan). Likewise, they do not provide training or business support.

4.3.3 Payday Loans Toronto

Payday Loans in Toronto are a for-profit company, offering small, short-term payday loans which can be used for any purpose including business. Loan amounts start at CAD100 to CAD1000 and is payable within 30 days. These organizations, around 200 in the GTA, serve those who have been turned down by banks. The approval is fast with “no questions asked”, even when the customer has bad credit. Regrettably, payday loans are creating a vicious circle of debt for those in need. The process is based on advancing money against a post-dated check that includes the initial loan plus fees and interest. The problem starts when after fourteen days the loan has to be repaid. When that period ends, the client pays the “lender in cash, lets them deposit the post-dated check or writes another post-dated check for the amount, plus an additional finance fee" (DiGangi, 2017).

4.3.4 Micro-lending offers

The mission and vision of these five organizations are the facilitation of microloans, up to CAD10,000, for small businesses or professional development. They supply loans to microentrepreneurs with outreach limitations. As previously discussed, almost 80% of microentrepreneurs do not know about the existence of microfinancing programs. The following are descriptions of the services, target market, and products these organizations provide to those living in Toronto.

- Access Capital Fund

Access Capital fund is a charitable organization that serves microentrepreneurs. It has more than ten years in the business, provides loans between CAD1000 and CAD10000, and offers business advice, if required. ACCESS clients are typically entrepreneurs who have been running a business less than two years and/or just starting a new business. The borrower may have no credit history or may have a poor credit record due to unemployment, illness, or unforeseen life events.

The client is required to prepare a business plan. The process starts after the customer has completed a business plan. The candidate is then interviewed by two loan officers in their business environment, home, or coffee shop. The loan officer presents a report to the ACCESS approval committee and in a united vote, they grant loan approval or decline the application. The committee gets together once a month or when there is a loan to review. Once the deal is approved, the recommendation goes back to administration to start the funding process through CIBC, a process that may take up to five business days.

The organization has served no more than 140 clients. This process can take up to three months from start to finish. Some customers do not follow through with the application because of difficulty filling it out or lack of business guidance.

- Black Creek Community Collaborative

The Black Creek Microcredit Program depends on Access Capital Fund to fund the loans. It is an appendix of the organization and targets small and emerging businesses in the Black Creek Community. The Black Microcredit Program was established in 2007 to provide loans up to CAD5000. Last summer, they launched a new initiative for high school students, college and university students who want to start and run a business with grants up to CAD3,000. They also offer free workshops and mentoring support. Its website provides a series of links to some local resources to complement the loans with active learning. However, after randomly selecting some links, the business pages were not found.

- Rise Asset Development

Rise Asset Development is a unique program created by the University of Toronto to provide low-interest business loans to those who are self-identified as an individual that has experienced mental health and/or addiction challenges. Participants develop entrepreneurship skills, gain practical tools and confidence while converting their business idea into a viable business plan.

The program offers loans up to CAD1500 to a diverse group of small entrepreneurs, ages19 to 29, wanting to start their businesses. It also offers peer-supported start-up programs and a series of educational workshops and mentoring that assist in the development of a business plan and entrepreneurship skills. The program occasionally grants CAD200 to those who complete the program and want to pursue entrepreneurship.

- Futureprenuer

This is a non-profit organization that provides financing, mentoring, and support tools to aspiring business owners aged 18-39. The requirements are a bank reference letter and a business that has been running just short of twelve months. Futurpreneur Canada supports young entrepreneurs with up to CAD45,000 in financing, an expert business mentor for up to two years, and resources to help plan, manage, and grow a business.

- The Ontario Catapult Microloan Fund

The Ontario Catapult Microloan Fund finances social enterprises that are already generating revenues and need to bridge cash flows and build credibility. Financing loans can go from CAD5000 to CAD25,000. This organization is a partnership between the Centre for Social Innovation, the Province of Ontario, Alterna Savings, Microsoft Canada, TD Bank Group, KPMG, and Social Capital Partners.

None of the micro-lending organizations mentioned above support business origination for low-income people in Toronto. None facilitate online applications or have a quick loan approval turnaround. They do not offer business training or financial literacy for entrepreneurs.

4.4 CONCLUSION

The challenges of microenterprise and microfinancing in Toronto are many. There is a lack of business fundamentals when starting a microenterprise. Even if someone wants to become an entrepreneur, there is little confidence to fully develop a social enterprise independent of donations and charity because of the lack of marketplaces or fear of penalty when people on social assistance are earning more income. There is a need for specialized assistance to access financial products and resources. There is also a strong need for a better classification of what is a microenterprise and a small business, so that people can look more closely at the sectors and provide more specific policies.

Table 12

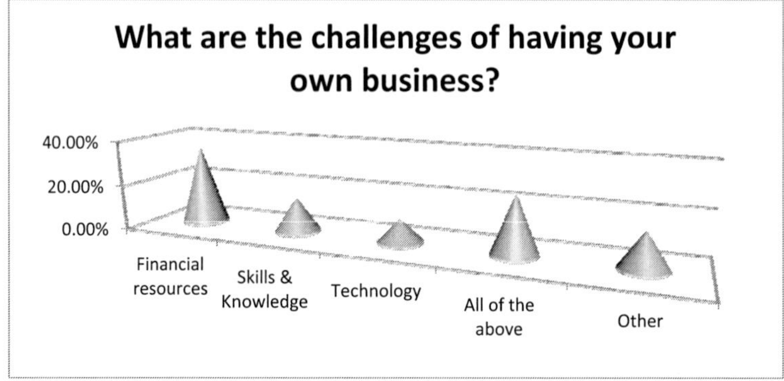

CHAPTER FIVE

5.0 CONCLUSIONS AND RECOMMENDATIONS

5.1 Conclusions

Strategies for alleviating poverty worldwide are way too many, but none has guaranteed a permanent solution. Some have strategies have reduced poverty levels. For example, microfinancing and microenterprises in developing countries have a positive effect in terms of empowering women and providing financial growth; however, in advanced economies, microfinancing is not vital to the creation of microenterprises.

In Toronto, five organizations provide microloans but requirements to access them are so cumbersome and discouraging that many entrepreneurs do not apply. As well, microfinancing companies do a terrible job at promoting their services; 85% of the local entrepreneurs surveyed had not heard of them, what they are, where they are located, and so forth. Hence, the use of personal lending products—credit cards, a line of credit, mortgages, or family and friends—have become the way to start a microenterprise.

Financing exists in many capacities with different products available for different types of businesses; with the sophistication of financial products comes the complexity of paperwork and expectations of what to expect from each financial institutions. Banks, online lenders, and angel investors are the most popular forms of small business financing. Consequently, entrepreneurs often need assistance to navigate those offers and prepare documentation, not just to obtain the loans but to skilfully guide the company toward continued growth and development.

Money or debt financing is not required at the initial stages of a business, especially in developing economies. The expectation is that micro or small entrepreneurs invest their resources at the beginning of their activities, and once they obtained annual gross sales of CAD85,000, that is when the business can apply for business loans from CAD5,000 to CAD35,000 for up to five years. Microlending companies may consider start-up company facilitating loans of up to CAD5,000 but the process may take 90 days in some cases.

Microenterprise is the backbone of Canada's economy. However, in cities such as Toronto, where opportunities to find well-paying jobs are more favorable than other North American cities, seeking committed immigrants or women to stick to entrepreneurship activities could be a challenge to be overcome. In the case of immigrants, the initial support to establish a business is none existent because settlement organization is not prepared for them. In the case of immigrant or single mothers that learn new skills as part of social development and want to start a new business, the idea of losing social welfare is terrifying. More awareness and reasoning about the possibilities of developing an income activity could do more than money in Toronto to continue building entrepreneurs and assisting people to rise above poverty. In other words, micro-scale business is underdeveloped and unattended. The Canadian innovation economy is not looking to empower micro-businesses. The need is for bigger in size and scale enterprises, ready to export and innovate. However, large-scale businesses could be supported by groups of co-workers associated with microenterprises.

Emerging social enterprises and the current demand for specific business knowledge, access to resources, financing and technology, demonstrate that resources are not getting to the target segment. There is a need for connecting organizations, that put together resources and community people, to build up the microenterprise environment. As a community, building social capital is required to serve the country and facilitate a way out of poverty. An individual who is not able to work should receive social assistance until they are ready to generate income as an entrepreneur or till they have developed trade skills that can guarantee the earning of money as a result of a business activity. It has been demonstrated that many immigrants, like entrepreneurs, are risk takers and can be bold in action if the right conditions are in place. Minimum wage paying jobs are not as attractive as opportunities to make more money but without being penalized. In the case of immigrant women, the fact that they are looking to supplement their family income is not only empowering, it is a chance to learn first-hand work responsibilities in conjunction with their family household tasks.

5.2 Possibilities and Recommendations

As demonstrated in the literature review, new entrepreneurship trends are developing and growing. The strength of microenterprises lies in its number. Ontario has more than 50% of enterprises in the micro and small business range. Government programs to support the business environment exist but access to them is cumbersome. When someone is finally able to decipher and unscramble forms and policies, and bring them to entrepreneurs is when entrepreneurs will step out of the shadow of mediocrity. Opportunities to grow and exist in local and international marketplaces should be created.

5.2.1 Mentorship

The implementation of mentorship mechanisms that create a synergetic relationship between existent resources at different levels of local and provincial governments and entrepreneurs is essential. The best alternative is to have a mentorship system that connects resources such as knowledge, specific trainers, resources, and funds, with the needs of entrepreneurs. Access to all the offers out there is a constant challenge for leaders of the WDN, for instance. For the Taste of Four Season Catering Group, a bigger kitchen for cooking and catering would represent an increment in business capacity. Available programs would not only provide them with training but with funds to improve the cooking facilities.

The relationship between mentee and mentor is base on a thorough understanding of the circumstances entrepreneurs face. In the present research, the targets that are the most vulnerable are immigrant entrepreneurs who are generating income with positive repercussion in their communities. The immigrant entrepreneurs that were interviewed, as well as the female microentrepreneurs from Regent Park are not homogenous groups. A mentor has to become a combination of coach and mentor which requires a careful assessment and approach depending on a person's background, race, language, motivators, business skills, or trade skills.

Training in entrepreneurship is difficult, but survey respondents are confident about receiving training and direct coaching. The WDN has received many business sessions from volunteers; presentations on pertinent topics occur when they pose a need. There is no planning ahead. When problems arise, they are tackled by people who want to help. Entrepreneurship skills could be developed when a successful match happens. For instance, when both a mentee and mentor share the same interests, background, and location.

A mentor is also a connector, one who builds bridges between entrepreneurs and local donors, government, and financial institutions with the range of existent resources. For instance, a mentor/connector can assist social enterprises to understand and access Ontario's Social Enterprise Strategy for the next five years, and to learn about the possibilities for development. A business mentor/connector is usually someone who had fought similar battles and won, and is ready to share their knowledge and open business opportunities for others.

Along with their daily operations, networking with like-minded individuals is a responsibility of great entrepreneurs. The mentor may guide or introduce new people, but the entrepreneur must network. They need to tell the story because people or possible customers respond to human connection and may also be willing to help.

A mentor needs to act as a coach responding to SMART goals (YourCoach, 2017). Many lack self-discipline and determination to stick to a plan. A mentor is the one who can keep the entrepreneur accountable and in line with goals. A mentor should be able to identify deficiencies and to be direct and upfront about what needs to be done for the entrepreneur's personal and financial growth. He becomes a supportive business coach to bounce ideas on.

5.2.2 Easier access to government programs

Current programs and services do not reach the target market. There is valuable information and opportunities to increase the development of small and microenterprises. However, to navigate the system is cumbersome and time-consuming. Even when the entrepreneur has learned about the individual program, just applying for it seems overwhelming: "I heard that there is a program that provides financial rewards to people that create microenterprises to come out of Ontario Work but I was not able to find it yet" (Paula, 2017).

The target for many government programs is the most vulnerable. Hence, it is the government's responsibility to make sure these programs reach the destination in an easy and accessible way. What is the use of having great programs if they are not communicated? It is necessary to build bridges that could extract and bring these existing programs directly to support social enterprises to achieve poverty alleviation goals? This is something that is worthy of future exploration.

Forms that are needed to access programs must be written in plain, straightforward language. They need to be easy to read, easy to understand, and simple to fill out. Also, the path to access these programs should be specified and easily reached. Otherwise, the many valuable hours of work it took to create these programs will be wasted, and neither the government nor the most vulnerable will benefit from them.

It is easier for low-income individuals to collect money from Ontario Works or disability support rather to look for ways to create business opportunities. Secure jobs are almost none existent. Government should create more environments to promote social enterprises to train youth and immigrants to match the market demands of the province. Self-employed and contract work is increasing but if the government supports entrepreneurship, a group of business networking analysts, for instance, could form an enterprise that would increase opportunities for negotiation.

There are no specific programs to teach low-income people how to get out of poverty. The government should provide guidance and professional consulting to encourage the creation of small enterprises that generate income activities complementary to social support. It is important to include workshops explaining entrepreneurship, and what a small business can do for them. Why is earning more money and declaring it is a better option than hiding it from the government? It is about teaching the basics of creating income instead of just providing social assistance. It is the fear of losing little things that control people's minds and having the comfort of receiving a monthly welfare check is good to many.

Non-governmental organizations (NGOs) and other community organizations should always identify and connect potential entrepreneurs with the right mentor in order to aid in the development of a successful business person.

Government should equip the not-for-profit sector with mechanisms for more direct and easy access to market development and microfinancing options. The current offers are insufficient and do not provide the full business training and financing requirements to grow a successful enterprise. The requirements to apply for microloans are excessive and discourage entrepreneurs from applying, thereby limiting the development of a person's full business potential. It is suggested that these programs find ways to simplify the process. For example, replacing the need for a business plan with a business canvas. In bullet point format or images, a business canvas offers a full explanation of what the business is all about. Compliance and risk go hand in hand; it is not just about giving out money. The right connector or mentor should be able to evaluate the plan of activities and make recommendations, as well as provide a higher weight for behavioral and previous business experience. Microfinancing organizations need to adhere to their mandate of providing business training and skills development in entrepreneurship. Existing programs currently develop employability skills but not business skills. Both financing and business training should be provided.

5.2.3 Marketplace creation

Toronto should take a leading role in bring together private and public companies to create market environments to promote local production. The opportunity to have a storefront for the display of merchandise is almost non-existent for small organizations. Community markets are becoming a significant option, but the aim is to have a more permanent marketplace. Entrepreneurs would be willing to pay for rental spaces is they were more affordable.

Toronto should be contracting more services and merchandise from micro-entrepreneurs and emerging social enterprises. It is about changing the mentality. It is about creating a direct way to provide an instant marketplace for small entrepreneurs.

With the intention of creating more stable neighborhoods, securing contracts with social enterprises and microentrepreneurs would allow the formalization of many small businesses. Small businesses are capable of providing quality services and products, but they are unsure of legalizing their activities due to fear of not having business contracts and not knowing where the next buyers are coming from.

The market environment also needs to create tax breaks for people that are transitioning from Ontario Works and Ontario Disability Support Program into social enterprises or small businesses. In this way, entrepreneurs would be able to save some money while improving and stabilizing their business.

Another alternative is to create online marketplaces for the commercialization of products or services. This would provide a quicker turnover for inventory. Current inventories for the WDN are from the last year's Christmas campaign; it is not because sales forecasts were inflated or too optimistic, it is because they did not have the right prediction for the market they went after. This group of ladies yearns for opportunities to showcase their merchandise. The fact that some market fairs only happen once a year does not create the sales they require in order to sustain the company. They need a permanent place to showcase their wares to the right target market and customers. For example, since the summer, the WDN has been using the “VIP room” at the Double Take store to sell their products and promote their services. There was no strategy in place, just the intention to experiment with the storefront. The group has not seen the results yet; however, with a market advisor, they could have spotted few variables that may reduce the impact of this activity. For example: The store sells second-hand items which the prices do not exceed CAD5.00. The merchandise produced by the WDN is priced three or four times higher and very specialized. The store is located in the Regent Park neighborhood on Gerard Street where there are not many walk-ins except for the neighbors. The room is a nicely decorated, and it is open to the public daily from 2pm to 4pm. The group takes turns working in the store and engaging with customers that are mostly their fellow citizens with similar demographic and income brackets. The average income in this area is CAD30,000, and probably, not many have a great desire for hand-made products that demand specialization and many hours of work.

5.2.4 Following new entrepreneurship trends

The traditional way of thinking about the workplace, job security, and the work itself has been changing over the past few years. Job places are coffee shops; job security comes with upgrading skills permanently. It is essential to look into trends to provide alternatives for people to create income activities as social enterprises or self-employment. It is impossible for government to provide job security for all Canadians. It is equally impossible for it to maintain social assistance for a growing number of recipients. What is needed is support for new business opportunities that offer training in specific areas that are vital to supporting an innovation economy. This includes business skills that teach new people how to survive working for themselves and creating new jobs for others.

The city should promote more microfinancing and mentorship opportunities for women located in neighborhoods at risks. It is activities for women that fill out the social enterprise spectrum in Toronto. They need a way to become successful at creating income that suits their abilities, time, family, and financial commitments. The system should find ways to reward people that get out of welfare and into self-employment or social enterprises by improving their financial and business literacy.

Small businesses and social enterprises are flourishing worldwide; hence, they should be promoted. It is time to create more job opportunities within the community and build capacity. Female immigrants find value in becoming entrepreneurs, as many have never worked before, and they have the chance to combine both entrepreneurship and motherhood.

It is recommended for government to define the types of businesses or workers required for the next twenty years and to promote the creation of micro or social enterprises in the communities for the provision of those. For instance workers or co-workers could easily create services or products to supply the current and future demand; the government secures the companies with contracts and has a direct impact on the economic development of the neighbourhood.

5.2.5 Collaboration and partnership

Last, civil society, private organizations, and government need to come together to assist in poverty alleviation. It is everybody's responsibility to take action in the economic development of their city and to bring a real and lasting economic change to their neighbourhoods. A dynamic transformation requires taking matter into our own hands. The goal is making sustainable and thriving communities to live in; a neighbourhood that everybody feels inclusive and proud.

Innovators, people with vision, or those running a local business should start enlisting the participation of bigger groups such colleges, universities, lending institutions, service organizations, and sole contributors, to aid in the development of their business or project. Initial steps could combine business and social capacity development. For instance, schools are to provide the necessary training to start a small enterprise, but this also creates a mutual developmental effect; students learns about social responsibility and empathy (dealing with low-income low-profile individuals) while perfecting their skills (Ranee, 2017). Lending institutions and credit unions can provide the administration, handling, and disbursement of loans. Service organizations, such as Rotary Club or Lions Club, could provide fundraising and donations, as well as the business and professional leaders to become the so much required business mentors (Louttit, 2017). Networking groups could start embracing micro-businesses but mostly they could create marketplaces and platforms to promote sales, meet likeminded people, suppliers, and partners. Using the same network of influencers, they can also strengthen direct government support and more investment for the communities movement; contracting directly suitable micro and social enterprises to supply products and services.

REFERENCES

Alliance for a Poverty Free Toronto, Children's Aid Society of Toronto, Colour of Poverty Colour of Change, Family Service Toronto, & Social Planning Toronto. (2015). *Toronto Child &Family Poverty Update 2015.* Retrieved from http://campaign2000.ca/wp-content/uploads/2016/03/Toronto-Child-and-Family-Poverty-Update-2015.pdf

Blackwell, R. (2015, November). Boomers will pass a small-business baton worth as much as $4-trillion. *Globe and Mail.* Retrieved from https://beta.theglobeandmail.com/globe-investor/retirement/retire-planning/boomers-will-pass-a-small-business-baton-worth-as-much-as-4-trillion/article27196152/

Bredberg, S., & Ek.S. (2011). *How to apply microfinance activities in the developed world. A case study in New York City.* Retrieved from http://www.diva-portal.org/smash/get/diva2:446575/FULLTEXT01.pdf

Bregman, R. (2017, April). *Poverty isn't a lack of character; it's a lack of cash.* Retrieved from https://www.ted.com/talks/rutger_bregman_poverty_isn_t_a_lack_of_character_it_s_a_lack_of_cash?utm_source=linkedin.com&utm_medium=social&utm_campaign=tedspread

Buckland,J. (2012). *Hard Choices.financial exclusion, fringe banks, and poverty in urban Canada.* (1st ed.)

Business Dictionary. (n.d.). *Entrepreneurship.* Retrieve from http://www.businessdictionary.com/definition/entrepreneur.html

Bygrave, W. & Zacharakis, A. (Eds.). (2010). *The Portable MBA in Entrepreneurship* (4th ed.). Hoboken, NJ: John Wiley & Sons, Inc.

Calabrese, D. (2014, October). A snapshot of Toronto: 51% of residents we born outside Canada, vital signs report finds. *National Post*. Retrieved from http://nationalpost.com/news/a-snapshot-of-toronto-51-of-residents-were-born-outside-canada-vital-signs-report-finds

Canada. (2017). *Canada's Innovation and Skills Plan*. Retrieved from http://www.budget.gc.ca/2017/docs/themes/Innovation_en.pdf

Canadian Press. (2017). Canada adds 48,399 jobs to economy in January: Statcan. *The TorontoStar*. Retrieve from https://www.thestar.com/business/2017/02/10/canada-adds-48300-jobs-to-economy-in-january-statcan.html

Cao, L. (2012). *Rethinking Microfinance*. Retrieved from http://scholarship.law.upenn.edu/cgi/viewcontent.cgi?article=1069&context=jil

Chapman, L. (2014, June). Luis Angarita, de caricaturista social a innovador solidario. *Radio Canada International*. Retrieved from http://www.rcinet.ca/es/2014/06/22/luis-angarita-de-caricaturista-social-a-innovador-solidario/

City of Toronto. (2016). *Toronto Strong Neighbourhood Strategy 2020*. Retrieved from http://www1.toronto.ca/City%20Of%20Toronto/Social%20Development,%20Finance%20&%20Administration/Shared%20Content/Strong%20Neighbourhoods/PDFs/TSNS2020actionplan-access-FINAL-s.pdf

City of Toronto. (n.d.). *TO Prosperity: Toronto Poverty Reduction Strategy*. Retrieved from https://www1.toronto.ca/City%20Of%20Toronto/Social%20Development,%20Finance%20&%20Administration/Strategies/Poverty%20Reduction%20Strategy/PDF/TO_Prosperity_Final2015-reduced.pdf

Community-Wealth.org. (2015, December). A city with opportunities for all: Toronto, Canada. The Canadian CED Network. Retrieved from https://www.ccednet-rcdec.ca/en/blog/2016/01/06/city-opportunities-all-toronto-canada

Cox, M. (n.d.). *Creative Destruction.* Retrieve from

http://www.econlib.org/library/Enc/CreativeDestruction.html

DEKI. (2017). About microfinance. *DEKI*. Retrieved from https://www.deki.org.uk/about-microfinance/?gclid=Cj0KEQjw4fy_BRCX7b6rq_WZgI0BEiQAl78ndzHB8VYk4c3V5tY5jXmJX15fEFe7Yk2077r5V8jO-SoaAlJB8P8HAQ

Development Today. (2017). Private sector development: Two simple guidelines. *Development Today*. Retrieved from http://www.development-today.com/magazine/2011/dt_2/opinion/private_sector_development_two_simple_guidelines

DiGangi, C. (2017, May). The truth about payday loans. *Credit.com*. Retrieved from https://www.credit.com/loans/loan-articles/the-truth-about-payday-loans/

Echavez, C., Zand, S, & Bagaporo, J. (2012, June). *The Impact of Microfinance Programmes on Women's Lives: A Case Study in Balkh Province.* Retrieve from http://www.refworld.org/pdfid/50f7b7b02.pdf

Economist. (2009, April). Entrepreneurship. *The Economist.* Retrieved from http://www.economist.com/node/13565718

Economist. (2017, February). Immigrants are bringing entrepreneurial flair to Germany. *The Economist.* Retrieved from https://www.economist.com/news/europe/21716053-while-native-germans-are-growing-less-eager-start-businesses-new-arrivals-are-ever-more

Economist. (2016, October). More slowdown than startup. *The Economist.* Retrieved from https://www.economist.com/news/britain/21708708-fears-future-one-economys-most-successful-sectors-more-slowdown-startup

Emery, H., & Ferrer, A. (2010, March). *The Social Rate of Return to Investing in Character: An Economic Evaluation of Alberta's Immigrant Access Fund Microloan Program.* Retrieved from http://www.iafcanada.org/wp-content/uploads/2015/10/The-Social-Rate-of-Return-to-Investing-in-Character.pdf

Entrepreneursunite.co. (2017). What is entrepreneurs unite? *EventBrite Events.* Received from https://entrepreneursunite.co.uk/

Financial Accountability Office of Ontario. (2017, September). Assessing the economic impact of Ontario's proposed minimum wage increase. *FAO: Financial Accountability Office of Ontario.* Retrieved from http://www.fao-on.org/en/

Finance Cosmos. (2009, July). Concept of joint liability group in microfinance. *Finance Cosmos*. Retrieved from https://financecosmos.wordpress.com/2009/07/19/concept-of-joint-liability-group-in-microfinance/

Financial Post. (2017). Personal finance. *Financial Post*. Retrieved from http://www.financialpost.com/personal-finance/rates/loans-personal.html

Food and Agricultural Organization of the United Nations. (2005). *Microfinance and forest-based small-scale enterprises*. FAO Corporate Document Repository. Retrieved from ftp://ftp.fao.org/docrep/fao/008/a0226e/a0226e00.pdf

Frankiewickz, C. (2001, April). *Calmeadow Metrofund: A Canadian Experiment in Sustainable Microfinance*. Retrieved from http:///www.calmeadow.com/metrofund.pfd

Futureof businesssurvey.org. (2017). *Future of Business Survey*. Retrieved from https://eu.futureofbusinesssurvey.org/manager/Storyboard/RHViewStoryBoard.aspx?RId=%C2%B3&RLId=%C2%B3&PId=%C2%B1%C2%B8%C2%B2%C2%B6%C2%B6&UId=%C2%B5%C2%B6%C2%B2%C2%B9%C2%BA&RpId=3

Giusti,C. & Estevez,L. (2011). Microlending for housing in the United States. A case study in colonias in Texas. Retrieve from https://www.researchgate.net/publication/257053329_Microlending_for_housing_in_the_United_States_A_case_study_in_colonias_in_Texas

Global Envision. (2006). The basics on microfinance. *Global Envision*. Retrieved from https://www.globalenvision.org/library/4/1061

Gomez, R., & Santor, E. (2001). Membership has its privileges: The effect of social capital and neighborhood characteristics on the earnings of microfinance borrowers. *Canadian Journal of Economics*, 34(4), 943-966.

Government of Canada. (2017). Statistics Canada. *Government of Canada*. Retrieved from http://www.statcan.gc.ca/tables-tableaux/sum-som/l01/cst01/lfss04f-eng.htm

Government of Canada. (2017). Budget 2017: Building a strong middle class. *Government of Canada*. Retrieved from http://www.budget.gc.ca/2017/home-Accueil-en.html

Government of Canada. (2017). *Canada's Innovation and Skills Plan*. Retrieved from http://www.budget.gc.ca/2017/docs/themes/Innovation_en.pdf

Government of Canada. (2012, July). Small business branch: Key small business statistics. *Industry Canada*. Retrieved from https://www.ic.gc.ca/eic/site/061.nsf/vwapj/KSBS-PSRPE_July-Juillet2012_eng.pdf/$FILE/KSBS-PSRPE_July-Juillet2012_eng.pdf

Government of Canada. (2015). Small, medium-sized and large businesses in the Canadian economy: Measuring their contribution to gross domestic product in 2005. *Statistics Canada*. Retrieved from http://www.statcan.gc.ca/pub/11f0027m/2011069/part-partie1-eng.htm

Government of Canada. (2016, June). *Key Small Business Statistics – June 2016*. Retrieved from https://www.ic.gc.ca/eic/site/061.nsf/vwapj/KSBS-PSRPE_June-Juin_2016_eng.pdf/$FILE/KSBS-PSRPE_June-Juin_2016_eng.pdf

Government of Canada. (2017, July). *Minister Chagger delivers keynote address at the She-Era 2017 Global Conference on Women and Entrepreneurship.* Retrieved from https://www.canada.ca/en/innovation-science-economic-development/news/2017/07/minister_chaggerdeliverskeynoteaddressattheshe-era2017globalconf.html

Government of Ontario. (2017). Minimum wage increase. *Ontario*. Retrieved from https://www.ontario.ca/page/minimum-wage-increase

Government of U.S.A. (2006). Chapter 95 – Microenterprise Technical assistance and capacity building program. United States. Retrieve from

https://www.gpo.gov/fdsys/pkg/USCODE-2010-title15/html/USCODE-2010-title15-chap95.htm

Guntz, S. (2011). *Sustainability and Profitability of Microfinance Institutions*. Retrieve from https://www.noexperiencenecessarybook.com/1lq7/sustainability-and-profitability-of-microfinance-institutions.html

Happy Healthy Women. (2017). *Happy Healthy Women*. Retrieved from http://www.happyhealthywomen.ca/

Harris, K. (2017 March 08). *Justin Trudeau marks International Women's Day with $650M for reproductive rights.* Retrieve from http://www.cbc.ca/m/touch/politics/story/1.4014841

Hudson, R. (2011, July 13-15). *The Regional Problem and the Social Economy: Developmental Potential and Limits* (Unpublished). Conference on Sustainable Community Business, Cape Breton University, Sydney, Nova Scotia, Canada.

Investopedia. (2017). Microfinance. *Investopedia*. Retrieved from http://www.investopedia.com/terms/m/microfinance.asp

Iganiga, B.O. (2008) *Much Ado About Nothing: The Case of the Nigerian Microfinance Policy Measures, Institutions and Operations.* Retrieved from http://citeseerx.ist.psu.edu/viewdoc/download?doi=10.1.1.492.2511&rep=rep1&type=pdf

Karam Kitchen. (2017). *Karam Kitchen: The Generous Kitchen.* Retrieved from https://www.karamkitchen.com/

Karnani, A. (2007). Microfinance misses its mark. *Stanford Social Innovation Review*. Retrieved from https://ssir.org/articles/entry/microfinance_misses_its_mark

Khanna, P. (2015, October). Global poverty: This is how to really reduce it. *CNN*. Retrieved from http://www.cnn.com/2015/10/05/opinions/khanna-global-poverty/index.html

King, L. (2017, April 17). *Entrepreneurship: The world is paying attention* [Web log comment]. Retrieved from http://www.huffingtonpost.com/laiza-king-/entrepreneurship-the-worl_b_9693094.html

Kumar, S. (2011). *Book review: Why doesn't microfinance work* [Review of the book Why Microfinance Doesn't Work, M. Bateman]. Retrieve from ///C:/Users/Owner/Downloads/Book_Review_Why_Doesnt_Microfinance_Work.pdf

Landau, E. (Ed.). (n.d.). Money. *Toronto Life*. Retrieved from https://torontolife.com/money/

Lawrence, D. (2017, March). Study shows the power of entrepreneurship training programs for women, minorities. *Globe and Mail.* Retrieved from http://www.theglobeandmail.com/report-on-business/careers/business-education/study-shows-the-power-of-entrepreneurship-training-programs-for-women-minorities/article34311628/?utm_medium=Newsletter&utm_source=Morning%20Business%20Briefing&utm_type=text&utm_content=MorningBusinessBriefing&utm_campaign=##mailinglogid##

MacDonald, C. (2014, September). *Entrenched and (Un)spoken: Neoliberalism and Canadian Microfinance.* Retrieved from https://qspace.library.queensu.ca/bitstream/handle/1974/12484/Clow_Erin_MM_201409_PhD.pdf?sequence=1&isAllowed=y

Mayoux, L. (2001). *Jobs, Gender and Small Enterprises: Getting the Policy Environment Right.* Retrieved from http://www.ilo.org/public/libdoc/ilo/2001/101B09_94_engl.pdf

Microfinanceinfo.com. (n.d.). *Microfinance and Microcredit.* Retrieved from http://www.microfinanceinfo.com/microfinance-products/

Minsky, A. (2017, June). Average hourly wages in Canada have barely budged in 40 years. *Global News.* Retrieved from https://globalnews.ca/news/3531614/average-hourly-wage-canada-stagnant/

Melhe, A (2015,February). Canadians want work. Why so many stopped looking?. *Global News.* Retrieve from https://globalnews.ca/news/1797379/canadians-want-work-why-have-so-many-stopped-looking/

Mjøs, O. (2006) . Award ceremony speech. *Nobelprize.org.* Retrieved from http://www.nobelprize.org/nobel_prizes/peace/laureates/2006/presentation-speech.html

Moore, D., & Buttner, H. (1998). *Moving Beyond the Glass Ceiling*. Thousand Oaks, CA: Sage Publications Inc.

National Immigrant Forum. (2016, December). *Immigrants sharing homes: Opening doors to opportunity.* Retrieved from https://www.airbnbcitizen.com/wp-content/uploads/2016/12/Airbnb_Home-Sharing_Full_Report_Final-WEB.pdf

Naudé, W. (2011). *Entrepreneurs and Economic Development.* Retrieved from https://unu.edu/publications/articles/are-entrepreneurial-societies-also-happier.html

Nobelprize.org. (2006). The Nobel peace prize for 2006. *Nobelprize.org.* Retrieved from https://www.nobelprize.org/nobel_prizes/peace/laureates/2006/press.html

Noor, K. (2008). Case Study: A strategic research methodology. *American Journal of Applied Sciences*, 5 (11), 1602-1604. Retrieve from http://docsdrive.com/pdfs/sciencepublications/ajassp/2008/1602-1604.pdf

OECD. (2006). *OECD Territorial Reviews Competitive Cities in the Global Economy.* Retrieved from https://www.oecd.org/gov/37839981.pdf

OCED. (2017). *Entrepreneurship at a Glance 2017.* Retrieved from http://www.oecd.org/industry/entrepreneurship-at-a-glace-22266941.htm

Parliament of Canada. (2017). House of Commons Canada: Bill C-25. *Parliament of Canada.* Retrieved from http://www.parl.ca/DocumentViewer/en/42-1/bill/C-25/first-reading

Pedrini M., Bramanti V., Minciullo M., & Ferri L. (2016). Rethinking microfinance for developed countries. *Journal of International Development*, 28, 281-302. Universita Catholica del Sacro Cuore, ALTIS, Milan, Italy

Perron, J. (2016). *Microfinance Barometer 2016.* Retrieved from http://www.convergences.org/wp-content/uploads/2016/09/BMF-EN-FINAL-2016-Version-web.pdf

Pratt, B. (2014). Payday loans: 600% interest rates. *Young Money.* Retrieved from http://finance.youngmoney.com/credit_debt/credit_basics/Payday_loans/

Putnam, R. (2001). *Social Capital: Measurement and Consequences.* Retrieved from http://smg.media.mit.edu/library/putnam.pdf

Rebekah J. (2010). Exploring women's participation in a U.S. Microcredit program. *Journal of Nursing Scholarship*, 42(3), 270-277.

Reynolds, C., & Novak, C. (2011, May). Low Income Entrepreneurs and their Access to Financing in Canada, especially in the Province of Québec/City of Montréal. Retrieved from https://www.microfinancegateway.org/sites/default/files/mfg-en-paper-low-income-entrepreneurs-and-their-access-to-financing-in-canada-especially-in-the-province-of-quebeccity-of-montreal-may-2011.pdf

Schreiner, M. & Woller, G. (2003). Microenterprise development programs in the United States and in the developing world. *World Development*, 31(9), 1567-1580.

Schnurr, J. (2017). Wynne government announces $15/hour minimum wage. *CTV news*. Retrieve from http://ottawa.ctvnews.ca/wynne-government-announces-15-hour-minimum-wage-1.3436150?autoPlay=true

Servon, L. (1996). Why loans won't save the poor. *Inc.com*. Retrieved from https://www.inc.com/magazine/19960401/1618.html

Shecter, B. (2015, November). CIBC forges 'fintech' partnership that will offer faster loans to compete with online lenders. *Financial Post*. Retrieved from http://business.financialpost.com/news/fp-street/cibc-forges-fintech-partnership-that-will-offer-faster-loans-to-compete-with-online-lenders

Shum, D. (2017, September). Ontario minimum wage hike will result in loss of 50k jobs: provincial watchdog. *Global News*. Retrieved from https://globalnews.ca/news/3736740/ontario-minimum-wage-hike-job-losses/

Sim, D. (2015, December). *Immigrant Entrepreneurship in Canada*. Retrieved from http://www.hireimmigrants.ca/wp-content/uploads/Immigrant_Entrepreneurship_Canada.pdf

Soy,S. (1998). *The Case Study as a Research Method.* Retrieve from http://faculty.cbu.ca/pmacintyre/course_pages/MBA603/MBA603_files/The%20Case%20Study%20as%20a%20Research%20Method.pdf

Spotton Vusabino, B (2006). Different and unequal: Payday loans and microcredit in Canada.

Journal of Economic Asymmetries, 5(1), 109-123.

Stegman, M. (2007). Payday lending. *Journal of Economic Perspectives*, 21(1), 169-190. Retrieved from http://staging.community-wealth.org/sites/clone.community-wealth.org/files/downloads/article-stegman.pdf

Storm,M. (2008). Transitioning from employee to entrepreneur. A road map for aspiring entrepreneurs. (2nd e.d.) paperback.

Tasan-Kok, T., & van Kempen, R. (2016, September). *Creating social cohesion, social mobility and economic performance in today's hyper-diversified cities.* Retrieved from https://ec.europa.eu/research/social-sciences/pdf/conferences/migration_2015/4_divercitiess_eu_presentation-ttk-vshort_160915.pdf

Toronto Public Library. (2017). Law at the library. *Toronto Public Library*. Retrieved from http://www.torontopubliclibrary.ca/programs-and-classes/featured/law-at-the-library.jsp

Tobocam, S. (2015). *Guide to immigrant economic development.* Retrieve from https://www.welcomingamerica.org/sites/default/files/wp-content/uploads/2015/06/Guide-to-Immigrant-Economic-Development_Final.pdf

USAID, (2002). *Decent work and the informal economy.* Retrieve from http://www.ilo.org/public/english/standards/relm/ilc/ilc90/pdf/rep-vi.pdf

Wayland, S. (2011, December). Immigrant Self-Employment and Entrepreneurship in the GTA: Literature, Data, and Program Review. Retrieved from http://metcalffoundation.com/wp-content/uploads/2011/12/immigrant-self-employment-and-entrepreneurship.pdf

Wood, M. (Producer), & Meier, T. (Director). (2016). *A New Economy* [Documentary]. Canada: Domain7 Studios.

Woman's Development Network. (2017. *Woman's Development Network.* Retrieved from https://www.facebook.com/wdnregpark/

World Bank. (2013, July). Supporting Entrepreneurship and Access to Microfinance for Morocco's Youth. *The World Bank.* Retrieved from http://www.worldbank.org/en/news/press-release/2013/07/25/supporting-entrepreneurship-and-access-to-microfinance-for-morocco-youth

Yunus, M. (2006). Muhammad Yunus - Nobel lecture. *Nobelprize.org*. Retrieved from http://www.nobelprize.org/nobel_prizes/peace/laureates/2006/yunus-lecture-en.html

APPENDICIES

Appendix A

Appendix B

Appendix C

Appendix D

Appendix E

Appendix F

Appendix B : In-depth Interview Guide – Leaders of Women Development Network

Demographics:

1. Background
2. Education level
3. Experience
4. Age
5. Married… How many kids…
6. What does husband do?
7. What kind of job did you do back home in ….?

Family economics before micro-enterprise

8. How is the money managed and distributed at home?
9. How is the interaction between husband and wife money wise?
10. How was the family dynamics before the microenterprise?
11. Is there a change after you become more involve in sewing club

Women's sewing group

1. Is this a full-time activity?
2. How did you become involve?
3. What do you produce?
4. Are you aware of the market needs and its potential?
5. What is the creative process?
6. How is your daily operations? – how many xxx do you produce?
7. Who set the price of your product? How?
8. Do you sell cash only or use merchant services?
9. How do you access to working capital?
10. Where do you get financing to start the business? How was the process?

11. How much money do you request? How much you got?
12. How did you use the money lend?
13. What is the perception that you have about your job? ....
14. Would you consider your business would be profitable enough to provide a source of income?
15. What is the main reason for you to do this job?
16. What kind of technologies do you use?

About micro-enterprise needs:

1. Do you think your role as income source has the same value here in Toronto than in.....?
2. Would you like to increase your business?
3. What would you require to be successful in your micro-enterprise?

About the future

1. How do you see yourself in the next five years?

Appendix C : In-depth Interview Guide – Business owners

Interview guide – Micro-entrepreneurs

Demographics

Name………………………………………….. Age……………. Gender F M

Biz Name……………………………………….When did you found it?.............

Employees…………..Annual revenues ………………….. Annual profit…………...

1. What business are you in?
2. Are you formally registered?
3. Do you have an internet presence?
4. Do you have or need a business plan?
5. Would you consider going online for business education?
6. What are your financing needs?
7. Have you applied for loans? Where? Did you get financing?
8. Have you heard about microfinancing organization in Toronto? Where? How? Have you applied? Why not?
9. Have you gotten any business training? Where?
10. What are your financing needs? How much? What have been obstacles/challenges to obtaining loans and getting training?
11. What could things be done better?
12. What would you recommend? What kind of services you need? Do you like evenings online training? Or rather in person training? How about training at a local library? What didn't work?

Appendix D : Survey invitation letter & Questionnaire

Interview guide – Micro-entrepreneurs

Email Invitation Details

Survey:	ME & MF survey (5766457)
From :	Romy.alegria@gmail.com
Subject	Survey Invitation
Email Mode	Plain Text

You are invited to participate in our survey "What are the challenges, barriers, and possibilities of the Microenterprises and Micro-financing in the city of Toronto". In this survey, approximately fifty people will be asked to complete a survey that asks questions about product knowledge, market, and business skills. It will take approximately ten minutes to complete the questionnaire.

Your participation in this study is completely voluntary. There are no foreseeable risks associated with this project. However, if you feel uncomfortable answering any questions, you can withdraw from the survey at any point. It is very important for us to learn your opinions.

Your survey responses will be strictly confidential and data from this research will be reported only in the aggregate. Your information will be coded and will remain confidential. If you have questions at any time about the survey or the procedures, you may contact Romy Alegria at 416. 278. 2540 or by email at the email address specified below.

Thank you very much for your time and support. Please start with the survey now by clicking on the Continue button below.

<SURVEY_LINK>

Please contact Romy.alegria@gmail.com with any questions.

Thank You

SURVEY

Contact Information Q01-C13

Name :

Business name :

Neighborhood/location :

Annual revenues :

*** What business are you in?**

Are you formally registered as?

Have you received any business training?

No

Yes

Where?

Would you consider going online for business education?

Yes

No

Maybe

How would you rate your knowledge of the industry you are in?

	1	2	3	4	5	6	7	8	9	10
Industry knowledge										

Do you have financial needs for your business?

Yes

No

NA

Have you received a business loan through micro-financing organizations?

Yes

No

Why?

Have you heard about micro-financing organization in Toronto?

Yes

No

Please rank you abilities on:

	1	2	3	4	5	6	7	8	9	10
1 Product creation										
2 Market needs										
3 Marketing										
4 Distribution										
5 Business knowledge										
6 Operations										
7 Industry Competition										
8 Financing										

What are the limitations to have your own business?

Do you believe having your own business could be a good source of income for you?

Yes

No

Please explain

What should be the city hall involvement to help you succeed in your business?

Printed by
Schaltungsdienst Lange o.H.G., Berlin